T0196457

Bowen's Road

My Walk Through the Fire

Cheryl Bowen Hance

authorHOUSE®

AuthorHouse™
1663 Liberty Drive
Bloomington, IN 47403
www.authorhouse.com
Phone: 1-800-839-8640

Published by AuthorHouse   5/4/2012

ISBN: 978-1-4685-9754-7 (sc)
ISBN: 978-1-4685-9755-4 (hc)
ISBN: 978-1-4685-9753-0 (e)

Libraryof Congress Control Number: 2012907562

Contents

Preface/Introduction

I am the oldest daughter of 8 children to Thomas and Rose Marie Bowen. I have seven siblings, three sisters and four brothers. I was born in Portsmouth, OH, but raised in a small town area called Owl Creek. I grew up on Bowen Road. There has always been a desire to write about the events in my life. I have always felt that sharing the challenges I have survived could help someone else to get through the pain. I am no one special. I know there are so many who have suffered so much worse in their lives. My hope, my prayer is this. I want the readers of this book to understand how I survived. It is my life and how I managed to grow and survive. I just have the desire to follow the Lords instruction to write this book. I have had many road blocks in my life that kept me from writing the book. The Death of my first husband Donald was the first adult road block. It sent me on a jagged path I never imagined I could recover from. This is a book of many trials and painful events in my life. They are all true with no added tails to make it more exciting to read. This book is a series of short stories from the first 56 years of my life. I hope and pray you the reader will understand I only want to offer hope in a world full of darkness! May God Bless each and every one who reads it! It comes from my heart and my love of Jesus.

Acknowledgement

I want to thank God first and foremost for pushing me out of bed and telling me to write this book. It was He who gave me the words and the strength to get through this process. He put the right people in my path to get this project completed. Thanks to my children Christina, Nathan and Tiffany for supporting me along the way. I love you so much! Thanks to Michelle Green-Seymore for supporting me. Thank you Beverly "Neicy" Garrett Morris, Paula Connell, my beautiful sister Eileen Boyd, and all my family for listening to me while I read you parts of this book and giving me insight on what I was doing. You have been an invaluable source of comfort during this journey. I love you. Cheryl

Dedication

First of all I want to give all the honor and glory to my Savior Jesus Christ. If not for you this book would not have been written. This book is to serve as testimony to the awesome glory of God and his love. God picked me up out of the darkest place I have ever been and placed a light to guide me back into his arms. I want to thank my parents, Thomas and Rose Marie Bowen; my siblings, Boyd, Raymond, Kenneth, Brenda, Emory, Eileen, and Loyce Ann for always loving me. You know all too well the pain I have suffered, because you suffered as well. I want my family and friends to know how much I love them, and I am so very thankful to them for all the love and support they have shown me all through the years. There are so many who have been there along my path in life. I want to thank Rev. Robert and Dorcas Lemon for showing me God's love during a childhood filled with sadness. The Owl Creek Mennonite Church located on Germany Road was a home for me when I needed shelter and safety. It brings nothing but happy memories for me. I love that little white church! To my children, Jeffro, Christina, Nathan, Tiffany, Charmaine and Frankie, and Barry; know that I love you with all my heart. You have been the bright spots in this life. Thanks to Donald and Barry for giving me the most beautiful children in the world. I will always love you!

Bowen Home

One thing I have learned in this life is that no one gets a free ride from pain and suffering! We are born into this life with a scream; a voice that begs to be heard, and the insatiable thirst to be loved! We need it desperately and will do anything to obtain it. The problem with that, is this, we usually go about it all wrong. We look to the wrong people the wrong things and take the wrong pathway. I can't speak for anyone but me. My life, this life God granted me has been filled with utter pain and disappointments. Having said that, I want my readers to understand how I got through all of it right up to this very day. I survived each and every trial with the love and protection of my Savior Jesus Christ. I hope the sharing of some of my challenges in life will be a real testament of how God has always been there for me even when I turned my back on him. My life, my struggle, my way, my pain!

Cheryl Bowen

The Beginning

I was born into this world as the oldest daughter to Thomas and Rose Marie Bowen. I am the oldest of eight children. There are 4 brothers and 3 sisters. I was born in Portsmouth, OH, but grew up in a little area called Owl Creek located in Pike County. I lived on a back road we refer to as a holler. The holler's entrance was a winding single lane dirt and gravel road. The road led to a dead end. The first years of my life were lived in a small log house that still stands today. That little house is located at the end of the road and sits just up on a hill. The log house was and still is surrounded by trees of all kinds and is tucked in by hills that surround it on all sides. The road that leads to the house winds along the creek bed. It seemed as though the road was made to follow the little creek. It is always lush and green in the spring and full of all kinds of wild life and birds. It was the perfect little picture. Pictures can hide awful things. I lived there with my grandmother Bowen, my parents, aunts and uncles and cousins. We were a very poor Appalachian family. We lived there until our little Blue three room house was built just down the road. The little house was built by my father, grandfather Hardin, and the local men in the family. There is one picture of mom and dad with mom's father standing in front of the house before it was finished. I still remember that old dirt and gravel road just like it was yesterday.

When you arrive at the entrance to the holler you are greeted by all types of trees that appear to be reaching across each side of the road to greet you. The trees form a cool shaded canopy to walk under in the hot summer days. I walked that road many days just to get away from home. The canopy provided shade and a cool breeze that gently blew through the trees and across my face. In the summer there was a heavy scent in the air of fresh wild flowers, such as orange Lilly's, purple irises, wild roses, and Daisy's. Black eyed Susan's and Queen Ann's lace flowers dotted the sides of the road. There was a nutty scent of the decaying leaves and broken tree limbs that had fallen onto the forest floor. I spent a lot of time on that old dirt road during my childhood. On those walks I could hear the dirt and gravel grind and crunch beneath my feet. It was quiet there, so each noise seemed to echo in your ears. The creek that runs beside the road offered its gentle symphony as it flowed across the small rocks and pebbles splashing along its way. The birds sat in the trees and sang along. Sometimes a rabbit would run out onto the road scaring us both. I busy with my thoughts, and the rabbit busy with his day. When our eyes met time seemed to stop for a fleeting moment. The rabbit was startled to see me there, and I had been awakened from a walking dream. The rabbit runs away, and I laugh because we had interrupted each others' events. I loved taking those walks and picking flowers. The sun was hot and the water in the creek cool and refreshing for hot tired feet. Every detail of that walk offered me peace and closeness to God. I have always felt closest to God when in the mist of nature. It was during that time in those walks I felt the safest and in the very presence of God. It was only when I returned home I felt unloved, lost, and so very alone.

Home is supposed to be a safe place isn't it? Looking back at my childhood my home was a place of fear, hunger, loneliness, and a profound feeling of emptiness, loads of hard work and responsibilities I should never have had to endure. There is a steep hill just behind our house. I used to climb it and sit there under the trees for hours just to get away from the house and all the siblings. Even in a house filled with a mother and father, and 7 brothers and sisters I always felt alone, unloved, and unimportant. The words I love you were never spoken in our house. Looking back that seems so strange. All those people there and no one told me I love you.

As I said I am the oldest of eight children. God saw fit to place me there, along with the help of my parents of course. As the oldest daughter I was my mother's helper. Our little 3 room house dad had built grew to burst at the seams. There was no running water and no bathroom in this house, and would not be until just before I entered into high school. That little blue house had one bedroom a tiny kitchen and a living room. The whole house may have been 900 square feet. That sounds big to me even now. Our home was heated buy a black cast iron pot belly stove. We burned coal and chopped wood obtained from the trees on our land. My mother cooked on a wood burning stove. She heated water on both stoves. We drew water from the well out back of the house. There were two creeks that ran along our house. The creeks ran along two sides of the house meeting at the back eastern side of the house and then flowed into one slightly larger creek. Those creeks were no more than 15 to 20 feet from our house. The road ran just in front of the house and a field at the back. We were surrounded. There was a wooden bridge that crossed over the creek in the back. There was the Out House, our bathroom, a chicken coop, rabbit cages, and a pig pen. During the childhood years the only other people that lived up this holler were my uncle and grandmother who lived in the log house located at the end of the holler, my aunt Bet and her children, my aunt Mary and Uncle Bob.

My mother depended on me to help her with my siblings. Mom gave birth to the eight of us in less than 10 years. I washed diapers in the creek bed using the rocks to help scrub them. In the early years mom had to use a scrub board that sat in a large round tin tube. We carried water in buckets from the well located just outside at the back of our house. We used that same tube to bathe in. The clothes were rinsed and rang out by hand and then hung on clothes lines in the back yard. I lost my childhood to helping my mother. I washed clothes, did dishes, I cleaned the house and baby sat. I learned to cook very early. I boiled baby bottles and filled them with fresh cow's milk. My childhood was not filled with books of wonderful fairy tales and grand castles sitting up on the hill. There we no long beautiful gowns or golden necklaces drenched in beautiful diamonds and emeralds. There were no handsome princes with the promise to take me away into happily ever after. No, my truth was filled with cold winter nights crowded into a bed with at least 3 of my sisters struggling to stay warm. The days were filled with hard work and hungry bellies. You see our father was unable to work as a result of an untreated illness that destroyed the valves of his heart. The 10 of us survived on less than $300.00 dollars a month from Social Security Disability. We survived on the eggs from our chickens, meat from the rabbits and squirrels dad hunted, and the garden we grew in the summers. My mother canned fruits and vegetables in the summertime. For most of the time there was very little to eat. There were many mornings mom made water gravy using saved bacon drippings. If we were really lucky and she had the flour, she would make what we called Cat Head biscuits and fried eggs. My mother made anything taste great. My mom made the best biscuit in the world! Friends of my father used to bring food to the house for mom to cook for them. Looking back I think it was their way of bringing us food without offending my father. They knew we had very little to eat most of the time. Mom made chilly, and the best sloppy Joes. The men would sometimes come early in the morning just to get her biscuits and sausage gravy.

The winters were the worst for us; especially when the fire would burn out, so we struggled to stay warm. The house always smelled of wood burning and sulfur from the dirty black coal. There was always dirt and mud mixed with wood chips and coal packed into the house by my brothers. The walls were browned with the smoke from the stoves and the cigarettes dad and mom smoked daily. It was worse in the winter. The wood and coal would be covered with snow that melted once put behind the stove. When we got hungry there were no gardens to sneak out to, and eat the fresh tomatoes or get ears of sweet corn to boil. It was a very difficult life! Our house was surrounded by steep hills and unclear fields. The dirt was hard clay and not easily tilled for gardens. We had to pack water in large buckets to water the gardens. Sometimes we were able to pack water from the creek beds. That was only if there was water in the creek to get. It was as if we had been dropped into a cavern and surrounded by hills covered by all kinds of trees. There was only one way in and one out! My father managed to purchase close to 80 acres of the land that surrounded us. It was our wonderland. We disappeared for hours in the woods. We made jump ropes from grape vines that hung from trees. We swung from the trees on grapevines and dropped into piles of leaves. We swam in the creeks while watching out for the local snakes. We had copper heads, poison water snakes, black snakes, as well as green and brown snakes to look for. We looked for tad poles and frogs, and turtles. We climbed over cliffs made of sand rocks. We climbed trees and disturbed bee hives. These were our toys! We were on our own most of the time. We would be gone for hours and no one looked for us. Our little house still stands today. My baby sister had lived and raised her children there. There have been many changes to that little house, but even today it only valued at $800.00 dollars for tax purposes, so even with the changes you can see it never grew up.

To this day when I look back on my life growing up on Bowen Road I search for love. Where was it? I never felt love there in that place. I never felt love from my parents or my siblings. All I knew was work and unwanted responsibilities. All I wanted was to get out of that place and run as fast as I could. Why should any child have to feel that way? No one ever ask us if we wanted to come here and suffer at the hands of so many for so long. Not only did no one ask me if I wanted to be here; no one warned me I would be neglected, abused mentally and physically and sexually, by the very people who were supposed to protect me. If I had been told about the life I would lead I probably would have ran as fast as the wind in the other direction! "But then GOD!" Yes, God said, "Yes you will be born, you will suffer my precious child in more ways than you can ever know. But I will be there to pick you up and carry you when you can't take another step. I will show you love, an unconditional love, a love so powerful you will one day thank me because I carried you through it all! Your life as horrible as it may have been is nothing compared to the joy I will give you if you only have faith in me." Praise God!

As a child I recall the throbbing pain of infected teeth, untreated ear infections, mumps and measles, burning fevers, and physical pain that never saw treatment by a doctor. We had no money, no medical insurance, and the closest doctor was over 30 miles away. If we had them, Aspirin tablets were placed directly on the cavities of the teeth that hurt, cigarette smoke was blown into infected painful ears along with warm sweet oil drops. Fresh open wounds were cleaned with rubbing alcohol. When we stepped onto an exposed nail with our bare feet there were no Tetanus shots to be had. God himself must have assigned a host of angels to guard over us.

The goal of this book is to reflect the love God has shown me, not the neglect I received from all those who were supposed to love and protect me. When we fail each other as we so often do, God will always be there to pick us up, and make us whole again! We just have to ask him to enter our lives, and except him as our Lord and Savior. We must give him our whole selves and make him first in everything we do!

The Fire

There have been so many times in my life that I have ask myself, as well as many others, and God himself this question, "Why God would you stand and allow all these horrific things to take place in my life." I have been given many different explanations over the years, but the life of Job explains it to me. I remember as a young girl going to church and hearing the story of Job many times. I also remember asking God for wisdom and the patience of Job. I had no clue at that time what I was really asking for, but I opened that door and God allowed me to walk through it.

God in his awesome grace gave us free will, and then he gave us his only son Jesus Christ to save us from the mistakes we will make when we chose the wrong path at free wills door.

JOB 5:7, Page 451, The Way the Illustrated Version, states: Mankind heads for sin and misery as predictably as flames shoot upwards from a fire.

Praise God! I see that in my life! I see it many times in many choices I have made with the gift of free will. I was a child in training; a child drawn to the fire. There was a desperate need to reach out and touch the fire, while at the time hearing my Lord saying, "Cheryl, you know better than to put your hand into that fire. It will surely burn you. The pain will be unbearable! I heard my Lord loud and clear, but the flames how they danced. The fire danced with brilliant colors of red yellows, greens and blues. They invite me in and offered warmth. The flames grew larger and brighter, and called out to me! God's voice drifts into the darkness. I can only see the fire now. I just wanted to reach out and touch the fires beautiful colors and feel the warmth. God's voice is now gone as I put my hand into the flame. At first it is magical and the warmth covers me. Then just as I surrender to beauty the agony rips and burns to my sole! I am consumed by it! What was once beautiful now burns at my flesh, and screams of utterly horrible and unexplainable pain burst from my every pore. My flesh melts like wax! I scream for God to have mercy on me. I beg him to pull me out of the fire! I made the choice to walk away from God's protection and into the fire. I was the stubborn child who disobeyed my father. I saw my Jesus cry bitter tears of pain as he watched me walk into that fire for he already knew all too well how I would suffer. All he could do was watch his child make a horrible mistake, but he stood there and prayed I would cry out to him for help, and return running back to him. Jesus walked through that fire and died a human death, so he could save our souls if we only ask him to. He will not remove the scars or the pain we suffer, but he will be there to heal them if we only ask. Jesus is a father with unfailing and all forgiving love! He will forgive all our sins if we just ask and chose to follow him.

That fire can be anything we chose to do outside of God's grace and mighty words of wisdom. I know there will be many fires that come our way in this life, and many of them we will have no control over; especially as children. Walking through fire is very painful, but it can also mold and shape us. It can make us strong and brilliant! We can go into fire as a lump of ugly metal, and come out shaped as mighty sword of God! But we have to allow God to be in control.

As an innocent child there were many times I was placed in a fire. I was sexually abused by a male family member. There is only one memory I can recall about the abuse, but it is enough to rip open my heart. I will not justify his actions by giving any of the details of the abuse. He is not worthy of any. That same man was also entrusted with the care of all of my siblings. He abused many in many different ways. To this day I have a small scar on my left wrist where he put his lit cigarette against my little arm and burnt me. God has protected me from other memories and I praise him for it. There are still times I feel a darkened cold wind blow across my sole. It's like those memories are trying to haunt me, but God will not allow it. I praise God for his protection. He alone knows how much I can handle.

The Fair

As children we were so very poor. We weren't really ever taken anywhere by our parents. There was just never any money to have fun. Every summer the fair came to town. The people from our small town all gathered to show off their livestock, vegetables, cakes and pies, as well as fruits and vegetables. It was a happy time, and a time to slow down, and enjoy the last of the summer. There were bright lights all around the fair, people met and caught up on the local gossip. Laughter could be heard from the rides as children and adults alike screamed with joy from the rides. Then there were the smells. OH the smells of fresh hot dogs and french fries, corn dogs, roasted corn on the cob and sweet fluffy colored cotton candy. There were bright red candy apples just begging to be eaten, popcorn popping and fresh lemonade. Sweet waffles dusted with white powdered sugar and fresh grown strawberries that burst in your mouth. Music played loudly from the rides and everyone screamed with joy. On this particular year I wanted to go so badly. I begged my father to let me go. My brothers had worked with dad on our sawmill, so they were going. I cried and begged to go. Finally he told me I could. I don't recall just how old I was at the time, but I did know men were looking at me in a different way now. I had no idea what that really meant. On this day dad allowed me to go to the fair with my brothers, but he only gave me enough money to get in. I do not remember even how we got to the fair, but I do remember what my dad told me. Dad told me if I wanted to ride any of the rides or have food to eat there would be a lot of men there. My earthly father put me in harm's way, but never taught me what to do in the matter of men. I was at least 13 years old at the time and in middle school. At some point I was on one of the rides, so I smiled and talked with the man who ran the ride I was on. He allowed me to stay on the ride as long as I wanted to. Then when it was his break time he asked me to walk with him. We talked as we walked along. Before I realized it we were at the back of the fairway where all the fair employees stayed. I was now alone with this man. To this day I don't remember what he looked like. All too soon I was down on the ground and this man had his hands all over my body and kissing me. I remember hearing God telling me to get up and run from that place as fast as I could. I broke loose from the man and ran! Once again my Savior protected me when man and my earthly father did not.

I do not recall my dad every telling me he loved me. I never remember him holding me or showing affection. Dad came across as a hard and cold man, but all the men and people who came around our house seemed to like and respect him. I know my mother loved him with all her heart. There were many who told me later on in life that my father was really proud of me. Why was he unable to tell or show me he did? I needed the love of my father so desperately. I still do!

Grandparents - Leslie T. and Myrtle Boggs-Hardin

Grandparents - Boyd Thomas and Christine Dace-Bowen

Exposure to Darkness

I recall one of my father's other attempts at showing me life as a woman. I was just 16 years old. One night my father and mother took me to a local bar with them. It was a small building filled with the stale smell of cigarettes and alcohol. Country music played loudly and people where sitting all around small round tables. I couldn't believe my dad had brought me to a place like this. What was he thinking? Was this his way of showing me how to have a good time, or was it an attempt to show me what happens to people who come to places like this. My dad and mom exposed me to people who drank alcohol until their words slurred and they could barely stand up. Some of the women there had men hanging all over them. My dad allowed me to dance with men who were much older than I. I do know in my heart and in my head I could hear a voice telling me to run from this way of life. This is not what I have planned for you little girl. Run as fast as you can from this way of life! Run as fast as you can. My dad never explained any of this to me. What was my dad thinking? I was always confused as young girl about how I was to act or what to do. My father took me to bars and sent me out on my own to fend for myself. But not once was I ever talked to about the ways of the world or how to protect myself. Dad never told me what to expect from men and mom just told me never to trust any man.

Cheryl Bowen

White Lipstick

This incident left me dazed and even more confused by my father. I was 16 and my best friend Sheryl and I were getting ready to go to a basketball game and a dance that would be held afterwards at our high school. It was 1971 and I was a freshman in high school. Sheryl and I spent the day together and got ready for the events to follow. We always had a great time together. We pressed our jeans and the white shirts we were to wear, and then curled our hair. Makeup was applied and we just knew we looked good! It was the early 70's and one of the new styles was to wear frosty white lipstick, so we applied it. At the time I had long thick dark hair. It fell down my back almost to my hips. I was a shapely size 9, and was blessed to have my mother's very large beautiful green eyes. As I looked into the mirror I always felt as though I was a pretty girl, but was always so insecure about myself. WOW, I wish I looked that way now! While Sheryl and I got dressed we could hear the voices of men talking to my father out in the living room. They were two local men who visited my dad often, and were well liked in our community. Once Sheryl and I were ready to leave we came out of my room and stepped into the living room. The two men stopped and looked at us like two deer that had just been caught in the light of an oncoming truck. That's strange I remembered thinking! My dad turned and looked at me. Then out of my dad's mouth came the words that crushed me! Dad said, "Get back into the bedroom and take that shit off your face. You look like a little whore." I was stunned! What did he mean by that, and how could he say such things to me in front of these men. I look like a whore! Stunned I turned and ran out of the room. As I ran out of the room I heard one of the men saying to my dad, "Junior, Why would you say such a thing to her? She is beautiful! Don't talk like that to her." That was the first time I ever remember any man defending me, and saying I was beautiful. He was also standing up to my father for me! At that moment on one hand I felt like a gutted fish and a princess all at the same time. I washed the lipstick off and left the house without speaking to my father. My dad never mentioned the incident and he never took the time to tell me what he really meant by what he said. He never ever told me he was sorry he had hurt me in such a way. Once I got to school I rebelled and put the makeup back on. Once again God provided me with a ray of sunshine in one of my darkest hours.

Battle Scars

In my whole life I have never felt like I belonged here in this world with these people. No matter where I have been I have felt alone and left out. I never seem to fit anywhere I go. There has never been a place or time in my life that I felt like I am good enough to be in that place, in that moment, or with the ones I was with. People seem to look over me like I am not even there in the same room with them. No matter how loud I screamed no one seemed to care about me. On the other hand I have always seemed to need them desperately! I wanted so badly to be loved and accepted, and to be needed and feel wanted! Their love and acceptance always seemed to be so much more important than the love of God. Sure I always knew God was there, and I knew he loved me. In my first 55 years of life He, "God", was always there waiting for me to call out to him. I always had God in my pocket, or in my purse, or even in the closet. God was always there like a warm blanket when I was cold. I never put God out front for all to see as the leader in my life. Oh how my life could have been different if I done so! God knows the path and the doors we will choose. He has the battle scars to prove it. Jesus has already paid the price for the doors he knows we will choose in our stubbornness! He died for the sins we have committed and the sins we will commit. We will be covered by the blood if we just ask him to forgive us and choose to put him first in our lives. We must choose Jesus! What a mighty loving God we can choose to serve! God knows we will be hurt badly by the choices we make and by the ones others choose to make against us, but he will glorify us in the end if we choose life in Christ. I now have made the choice to thank and praise God through the storms that rage within me! Praise God! I love my Jesus!

My earthly father never ceased to stun and to crush my spirit. During my freshman and sophomore year in high school I was the President of our 4-H club. It was a very small club at the time. There were only a few of us. One day a letter arrived to my house with an application to apply for the tryouts for the local Pike County Junior Fair Queen and her court. I looked at it but did not dare to fill out such an application. I was not a popular girl in High School and I was very poor to say the least. I put the application aside. A few days later I was visiting my best friend Sheryl. Somehow the application came up, and I ask her if she was going to fill it out. I don't remember her response, but I do remember what she told me when I said I was thinking about sending it in. We are still good friend to this very day, but she broke my heart on that day. I told her I thought about sending in the application but had changed my mind. Her response was this, "It is probably good that you didn't send it in. you wouldn't make it anyway." WOW that hurt! I never told her how much she hurt me on that day, but something rose up and stirred a fire within me. I was tired of being treated like I was nothing because our family was so poor! I went home pulled out the application, completed it, and put it in the mail box.

A few days later I received a letter from the 4-H and was informed I was to meet with the other chosen applicants at Pike County High School for the interview. I was thrilled! I was chosen. Then the doubts started to rise up. I have never been through and interview before. My parents had no money to buy a gown if by some chance I did win. If by God's grace I was chosen as even one of the 5 runner ups I would need a convertible to ride in, and a date to escort me there. There would be new cloths for me to wear at the events during the fair. I would be required to attend the fair everyday which meant I needed a car and gas to get there for an entire week. I had no idea how I would get those things. We had no money! Then I recalled our pastor telling us, When you go to the Lord and pray, ask it in Jesus name and you will receive an answer.

John 14: 12 – 13 My Bible The Way: In solemn truth I tell you anyone believing in me shall do the same miracles I have done, and even greater ones because I am going to be with the father. You can ask him any-thing, using my name, and I will do it, for this will bring praise to the father because of what I the Son, will do for you, Yes ask anything using my name and I will do it!

So, in simple faith in my Jesus: I prayed, "God, would you allow me to be one of the chosen five contestants? In Jesus holy name, Amen." I did not ask to be the Queen. The day arrived for the interview. I was so excited and scared at the same time. To top it off I woke up that day with a really stiff and painful neck. That did not deter me. I took out my mother's old brush hair rollers, I washed my long hair, and then spent an hour rolling it all up. I had no money for a new dress for this interview, but I located one of mom's dresses. It was very simple. The dress was sleeveless and form fitting. It was made from a stretchy polyester material; white at the top and navy blue at the bottom. The dress was a little too long for my liking, so I hemmed it just above my knees. I then washed the dress and hung it outside to dry. Once the dress was dry I ironed it. I was almost ready for the interview. I made a point not to tell anyone but mom that I had applied for the position. My thought was if no one else knew I had applied to the contest I would save myself the shame if I were never considered. The time came and I arrived at the school with mom. Once I arrived I saw several other girls I knew from our area, including my best friend. They were shocked to see me there! Then the doubts came rushing in. "What are you doing?" I ask myself? But it was too late I had been seen, and there was no place to hide. So, I took a deep breath and collected myself. We were all called into a large room. Our mothers sat there with all of us. You could feel the electric in that room. I was so nervous! Then the interviews began. The contestants were called in one by one for the interview. Then came my turn. I walked into the room where the judges were sitting at a table. A single chair was placed just in front of them. I said hello and sat down. To this day I do not remember a single one of the faces of the judges. I do remember two of the questions. The first question: What do you plan to do with your life and how will you serve you community? It was an easy question I thought. I took a deep breath and began. I told them I planned to become a nurse. I am currently taking college prep classes and I am a volunteer Candy Striper at our local hospital. The position allows me to be exposed to many types of people and careers possibilities that are available in the medical field. It shows me the nurse's roles in the care of patients, so I can make an educated decision about my career choice. Once out of college I want to work in the hospital I am now volunteering at. I want to get married and have four children. I want to be the best mother and wife I can be. I plan to help out in the schools as needed.

The second question however was like I had been punched in the stomach! I never imagined this would ever be a question in this type of contest. The question was: If you were approached by someone who was planning to commit suicide what would you do and what would be your advice? It was very difficult to get my answer out. You see earlier that year I had tried to take my own life. Thankfully I did not succeed. Once again God was there with me. I sat up straight and looked the judges directly in the eyes. I answered that question! My answer was this. I would tell the person their life mattered and even if they did not think they were important they were so very wrong. Each of us has a job that no one else can fulfill on this earth. If you chose to take your life no one else can replace you. There will be a whole in the world. Each of us has a job to do. It is also a very selfish thing to do. If you take your life you leave many unanswered questions. Talk to someone, anyone and ask for help. Your not alone. There are many people who have the same issue you may have. Choose life. There is nothing on this earth worth taking your life for. Whatever or whoever hurt you will still be here enjoying themselves and you will be gone. Who wins? Your life is just as important as theirs, so don't allow someone else to take your power away. I got through it. The judges thanked me for my time and told me to return to the room with the others. The rest of the contestants were called for their interviews. What took only about an hour seemed like an eternity? Finally the last contestant had been interviewed. We were all told to take a short break while they judge's competed their choices. We all walked outside. There was laughter and talk of frayed nerves. The door opened and we were told to return to the room for the results. My heart pounded! Then it happened. The judges walked into the room. You could have heard a pin drop it was so quite. One of the judges said, "We want to thank all of you for your participation. Each one of you is very special and would be a fine example to represent this community. But there are only 5 positions. The 5 ladies chosen tonight will attend the opening night at the Pike Country Fair. There the Queen will be announced. So having said that here are the five finalist's names, they paused and then I heard it. The first name is; Cheryl Bowen, I was the first one called! OH my GOD I screamed inside! I couldn't believe it! I looked over to my mother. There she sat with the tears just flowing. I was in shock! I never even heard the other four names as they were called. My Jesus had answered my prayers. I was so happy I thought I would explode. I was chosen. WOW! After all five names were called we were ask to come to the front of the room. For the very first time I felt like I was someone special! I had value! Grown professional men and women had looked at me and heard what I had to say and thought I was special enough to represent our county in such a public way. I was honored beyond what my words could express. Our pictures were taken and placed in the local newspaper. There I was on the cover page of our local news paper for everyone to see. I knew my dad would be proud of me now. I mattered!

The first day of the fair arrived, and it was time for the crowning of the Queen. All the things I had worried about in the beginning God supplied. I received a small check and so I was able to purchase the formal dress that was required to wear to the crowing ceremony. I found a dress for just 10 dollars and was able to purchase new shoes and a few outfits to wear to the fair. I was given the gift of a beautiful red and white convertible by a young friend who lived just down the road from me. It was a requirement to ride sitting up on the back of a convertible as we rode to the grandstand for the crowing of the queen. David and I had gone to school together all our lives. David drove my date, Robert, and I through the parade on one of the most exciting days in my life. Once again God provided when I just stepped out in faith and believed in his promise. I was the first to arrive at the grandstand. What a sight. The grandstand was filled to capacity and mom and dad were there along with so many of the people from our area. I was representing them and they were proud! I was filled with joy to be there for them. All five came on the stage. We were all introduced and the Queen was named. I was not crowned Queen that day but you could not take way the pride I felt on that stage. My God had given me what I ask for and I was too happy to care that another had been chosen into the number one spot. I did not pray to be queen. I only ask that I be one of the five. We were all placed in our ranks and the Local newspaper took our pictures. That picture was put on the front page. There I stood once again on the front page news for all to see. I was so happy. In all my years at school I was never made to feel like I was good enough for the so called popular girls. My clothes were not new and I did not have nice shoes or bows for my hair. I was made to feel unloved and un-excepted by my peers, but on this day I was good enough! As they say I was on cloud nine! Once all the pictures were taken and the congratulations were expressed we headed to the car to go home. We all talked on our trip to the car. I do not recall the content of all the conversation, but I will never forget what my father said to me once we got to the car. Dad looked at me and said, "I knew you would not be chosen as Queen. That girls family owns the local car dealership and she is prettier that you." In one fleeting moment my father took me from cloud nine with a bullet straight through my heart! My father pushed me off cloud nine with his words and allowed me to plummet to the rocks below! My father got into the car like nothing had been said. How he could he say such a thing?! Why would he hurt me in such a way! Aren't our fathers supposed to be our safety nets!? Looking back now I am sure he did not mean to hurt me in such a way, but he did! I was never going to be good enough in the eyes of my dad. If my own father didn't see me as a beautiful young woman then I must not be.

> *God gave me this passage: John 1: 11 – 12 Even in his own land and among his own people, the Jews, he was not excepted. Only a few would welcome and receive him…*

I was coming to understand I would never be accepted by my own people, because I am a child of Gods! There God was again, my Lord and Savior was supplying comfort.

My Suicide Attempt

Earlier I spoke of my attempt to take my own life. I will tell of that event. I was just 17 years old, and had just broken up with what I thought was the love of my life. I needed to feel and be loved so badly. John entered into my life early that year of 1972. I fell hard for the first time. I thought he was so handsome. John's car was the most beautiful thing I had ever seen! It was a 68 Dodge Charger with the colors of cobalt blue on the lower half and had a white top. The rear wheels had been lifted up and the sound of that engine was like music to my ears. I was a 16 year old teen who thought she had gone to heaven! My prince had come to rescue me. I was so very much in love and he made me feel loved for a time. He lathered me with gifts and took me out to movies and introduced me to his family. We double dated with my friend and her boyfriend all summer long. John was already out of school, and had a job. He still lived with his parents. I had known of John when I was a freshman, but his family moved and he attended and graduated from another school. I also knew one of his sisters really well.

John and I met once again at one of my school functions. I was singing in the chorus that sat just above where was seated. I remember looking out into the crowd and seeing him sitting there. His smile lit up the room. I just sat there and stared at him. Then he looked at me. I quickly turned my head. I was so shy when it came to men and didn't want him to see me looking at him. I never felt attractive enough. I looked over at him again and he looked back and smiled at me. WOW he is actually looking at me! He smiled at me! Oh the mind of a 16 year old! My heart was pounding and I could only dream of us together. In my mind it would never happen. But it did! John got my number and called me later on that week. I was so excited! At first my dad and mom would not allow me to go anywhere with John alone. I always had to be with another group or couple. I fell in love with John like a freight train going 100 miles an hour. He made me feel special. He made me feel loved. One evening after we came home from a date we were outside and I was sitting on the hood of the car. My mother walked across the road to where we were. She told John my dad had said he thought we needed to slow down. He didn't want us to move to fast. Dad did not come himself he sent my mother. John looked at my mother and told her to tell my father that it was too late. We were already in love! Mom just walked away. I was the happiest girl alive in that moment. That was the first time a man had ever taken up for me in such a way. He stood up to my father! The time finally came when I was allowed to see John all by myself. We could date without someone else along for the ride. John gave me his class ring. I wore that ring with such joy and pride. In that time it was the thing to do. We called it going steady. The guy gave his class ring to the girl he chose to commit to. The ring was adorned with angora string each and every time I changed my cloths. It was always to match my clothes. The angora string once wrapped around the ring was fluffed up and looked like a piece of colored cotton candy. Any girl who had one of these rings was considered to be in the popular group. There I was I had the ring and one of the most well know boys in the area. I was one of the popular girls now! All the girls wanted to see the ring and I was very happy to show it off. In this small town and school it was a tradition to exchange class rings with the one you dated exclusively. I was living the dream. I had found my prince, and as far as I was concerned it would last forever. He drove to school and picked me up, so I did not have to go home on the bus. It was so much fun to walk out of school with my best friend Sheryl and both us meet our boyfriends. Both the guys we dated had really hot Dodge Chargers. We climbed into those cars rolled down the windows took off our shoes and stuck our feet up on the dash. We would wave at the others as we zoomed past them as they waited on the bus to go home. It was a magical time for me! For the first time I felt like I was a live and in love. I attended church regularly and was a member of the youth group. I loved my pastor and his family. I loved my Lord! I had never had sex and did not plan on it until married. I became swept away with this love I had for John and I gave into him. He was the very first for me. Something strange happened to me the first time we made love. Once the act was over I felt funny. I had always been told it would hurt and I would bleed. None of those things happened. After John ask me if that was really the first time for me. I could not understand why he would feel like that. I was confused. Why was it as it was? I put in the back of my mind. I felt the guilt because I knew I was not to do this, but I was in love and I knew God would understand it. That was the lie I told myself so I could continue on with the relationship I had started with John. I loved him and I knew he loved me, or at least I thought he did. I am sure he loved me but not in the way I loved him. We were so young. John and I spent summer nights looking at the stars after making love. He held me and made me feel like I was the only girl alive. I gave my heart to John. I didn't listen to the voice of God anymore. I knew in my soul I was wrong but I did not listen. I was in love. John and I talked about our future, marriage and family. In my mind we would be together forever! As most first loves do ours began to fall apart. John started a new job and did not call as often as he had been. Then one day my parents came home from shopping. My mother told me they had seen John pulling out of the parking lot where they had just been. I was told he had another girl in the car with him. I made every excuse I could come up with. It could not have been him. He would not do that to me! You are wrong mom. I was frantic! She looked at me and said I hope so. I called John at his house and his job. He was not there. I called my best friend and begged her to have her boyfriend at the time come and take me to John's job. Finally they came. We drove the 20 plus miles to his job. We pulled into the gas station where he was. I ask him if he had been out with someone else, and then told him mom and dad had seen him. He told me he had not! In my heart I wanted so badly to believe him, but my head told me my mother and father would never lie to me about something like that. I drove off. I called John later after he got off work and we scheduled a date. When the date ended and he drove me home. We sat in the car just in front of my little house. It was not the same between us. I could feel the tension. So in my teenage way of communication at the time I ask John, "Are you sure you still want to go steady with me?" There was dead silence! He waited too long to respond. I had seen the difference in him. He did not call me as much anymore, and the dates were fewer and fewer. I put it all on the new job. I loved him so much. I did not want this to end. After the deadening silence I pulled of the ring, removed the angora and handed it to him. He just sat there. He didn't say a word. I was so hurt I thought my heart was going to burst right out of my chest. The tears began to flow. I gave John what he didn't have the courage to ask me for. I broke up with the man I thought was the man of my dreams. I opened the car and ran into the house. My world was falling apart. I heard John drive away. I cried most of that night. The next morning I removed all of his pictures and the stuffed animals from my bed. I thought if I removed all the visual things of our time together it would somehow make it better. It was like a deep black hole had been opened in my heart. I felt like I would never be the same again. I need to get out of the house, so I dressed and walked over 3 miles to John's sisters house. She and her husband had been friends to me before I knew John. In fact they were like another set of parents to me. I needed a friendly face. When I arrived John was there standing in front of the big red barn. I just wanted to run to him, but my pride would not allow it. He spent a lot of time there helping in the summer months bailing hay and anything else they may need. I could see pain in his face. He ask if we could talk about it. I looked at him and said there is nothing to talk about. I walked away. I wanted him to call out to me or run to catch me. He did not do so. I spent the weekend crying and in so much pain. Funny, my mother nor my father did anything to try to talk to me or show any type of compassion during this time of agony. I was on my own.

Monday came and I was trying to get ready for school. I was still devastated about the breakup. I was on the edge. During this morning my brother said something that pushed me over that edge. At this time I can't even recall what was said, or even what the conversation was about. All I knew was I did not want to live anymore in this pain. I was upset with my father. Why was he never there for me! I felt utterly alone and scared. I then decided to make them all suffer. They would see what it was like to hurt! I would see if my father cared about me or not. I then opened the cabinet where all the medications were stored. I pulled out everything I could find. There was Aspirin, blood pressure medications and other meds dad was taking. I remembered thinking I will just see if anyone in this house or anywhere else cares a thing about me as I swallowed handfuls of pills. Once I had taken all the pills I gathered my things and climbed on the bus to go to school. The pastor of my church was also the bus driver. He smiled and said good morning as he always did. I just looked at him. I did not return the gesture. I chose a seat and sat down. I wondered how long it would take to start feeling the side effects of the medications I had taken. How long will it take for me to die? I felt no one would care anyway and I just wanted the pain to go away!

A few stops later my friend Sheryl got on the bus and sat down beside me. My pastor kept looking at me from his rear view mirror. He knew something was wrong, but I would not talk with him. I was not talking to Sheryl either. She wanted to know what was wrong, but I ignored her for a long time. I was now starting to feel strange. The drugs were working. I leaned my head over onto the window. I didn't want to talk I just wanted it to be over. I wanted the pain to just go away. Sheryl finally got out of me what I had done. I didn't care! Once off the bus she ran and got her friend and they took me to the local hospital. I was taken directly into the ER and put on a bed. They attached an I.V. and started running fluids. The nurse taking care of me ask what medications I had taken. I told her as best I could. I started to cry uncontrollably. I wanted to see John. I was told John did show up, but I do not recall him being there. I did not want to see my dad and mom. My mother and father arrived to see me. They talked with the nurses, but never to me. My father just stood at the doorway. He never tried to talk to me or comfort me. He never tried to find out why I had tried to take my life. Afterwards I was taken home. Once there I went to my room and climbed into bed. A little later an uncle of mine came for a visit. I heard my mother tell my uncle, "Well you might as well hear it from me, Cheryl just tried to kill herself today. We just got back home with her. I did not hear the response my uncle made, but he too did not come to see me or offer any kind of advice or comfort. I was a scared teen and no one talked to me. No one ever talked to me about the incident. I guess if you don't talk about a problem there is none. I was so confused and so lonely! I felt abandoned and unloved. Life went on! Physically I was not harmed, but I was now even more closed off from everything. In my mind what I had attempted just confirmed what I thought. Just bury your heads in the sand and it will all go away like it never happened at all. I believe it was then I resolved not to ever trust anyone ever again. They didn't care anyway. The problem was I included God in that decision without realizing it. Actually until this very moment as I make this entry I realize when I made that very decision not to ever trust anyone I had placed a wedge between God and I as well. I told myself that God loves me, but I could not trust in it. I had decided that to love just cost way too much and I would never love that way ever again.

The Test

I began to challenge those who told me they loved me. I began testing people. I would see who loved me. Words meant nothing anymore. Words were just that and so easy to be said. I decided for the ones who told me they were my friend I would know from now on if they really were. If they didn't pass my test I shut them out of my life, and for the most part they never knew why I had treated them so badly. The first person I remember testing was the pastor of my church. He also drove my school bus, so he was an easy target. I was so wrong to do this to him. Rev. Robert Lemon and his wife, Dorcas treated me like I was one of their own. Bob as he was called always had a big beautiful bright smile for me each and every morning. He greeted all of us with a hello and how are you. For no reason I just stopped talking to him. It would go on for weeks. He still said hello and greeted me with a smile, but I would catch him looking at me through the mirror. He had a worried look, but he never ask me why. He never treated me any different. Bob endured this treatment several times during my High School years. He loved me anyway! Bob and Dorcas provided love and support. I was welcomed into their home always. They gave me a view into a home that had love and support for each other. Something I did not feel in my own home. Dorcas showed me how to cook and how to sew. She was and is a wonderful example of a Godly woman. Dorcas has a laugh that can fill up a room. They included me in some of their family vacations. Dorcas showed me more by example than any other way. Dorcas was the closest person to an angle on earth I have ever known. Dorcas was soft spoken but firm and supported her husband and children. She kept her home spotless, and she could make some of the best cookies I ever ate. Dorcas is a lady! Through their selfless actions I was exposed to what a God loving family could be like. To this very day I praise God for them. In their families I was introduced to men who worked and took care of their wives and children. They told them they loved them every day. There were hugs and kisses given freely. They sat down at the table and ate as a family. I wanted a husband like them! I wanted to be loved like that.

My "testing" also included my best friend Sheryl. Sheryl and I became best friends during the 6th grade. We are still friends today. Much like Bob I would just stop talking to her. Sheryl would beg me to tell her why I wouldn't talk to her. She passed me notes in the classes we shared together in high school. Even I really didn't understand why I did this. I was miserable when I shut them out. I missed them so much. They were my only safe place and I chose to shut them out. They always welcomed me back with open arms. They were my angels.

Love

I have learned this, because you love does not mean it will be returned to you. You will love in this life and it will either be returned to you or it will shatter your heart in so many pieces you may think you can never survive it! Just think about that. Remember the first time you gave away your heart only to have it crushed and returned back to you! Sometimes the pain is so bad you can barely breathe. It hurts so much you can't put it into words. When I think of all the times I have loved and it wasn't returned my heart became a little harder from the scars it caused.

Now just think how God must hurt! He gives his love and his heart to each and everyone one of us freely. We take his love and use it when we need it. We then drop his heart , we stomp on it when we don't get our way and then we toss it aside opting for human love. We think the love from a husband or a wife will fulfill our needs. We put Gods heart on a shelf to collect dust and dry up. We even forget we placed it there for a time. Then when the love we chose fails us we begin to look for the heart of Jesus. Where is his heart? Then we remember where it is. We take down the heart, dust if off and an amazing thing begins to happen. The heart of God begins to beat softly and then the more we cry out to God the heart begins to beat faster becomes full and beautiful in our eyes again. God's love begins to pour out and cover us. God's heart longs to show us love and happiness. God loves us and wants us to walk with him. Trust in him, but we have to give our lives and heart to him. We must always and in everything put him FIRST! We must choose life! He makes me whole in the presence of his glory! Isn't it amazing and truly wonderful. God wants us ever when we turn our backs on him and break his heart. God wants us to feel loved and cared for. He will always be there for us if we follow him. God gave me Psalms 23 while writing this message.

Psalms 23

I opened my Bible: The Way, The Living Bible Illustrated and began to read Psalms 23. In my Bible the wording I am used to is written differently, so I go to my mother's old King James Version. Our mother, Rose passed away March 24, 2011. It has been almost a year now. Just yesterday I was beginning to have doubts about writing this book. The voices in my head were saying to me, who do you think you are? No one cares about you and they sure do not care about your struggle in life! Everyone suffers. There are a lot more people who have suffered greater than you. I prayed that God would show me I was to continue with this book. I took my mother's Bible off the shelf and I walked to the table and sat down. There was one of moms cloth handkerchiefs placed in the Bible. I opened the Bible to the place the handkerchief was in. It was Psalms 23. I just cried! God gave me Psalms 23 and mom had it prepared for me. Praise you GOD! Thank you! You confirmed my book once again! I felt the Holy Spirit refill and refresh me in that moment! Jesus, Jesus, Jesus, how I love that name! Even my mother reached out to me this day.

The Holy Bible Kings James Version: red letter version: page 880

Psalms 23

The Lord is my Sheppard; I shall not want. He maketh me to lie down in greens pastures; he leadeth me beside still waters. He restoreth my sole; he leadeth me in the paths of righteousness for his name's sake. Yea, though I will walk through the valley of the shadow of death, I will fear no evil; for thou art with me; thy rod and staff they comfort me. Thou preparest a table before me in the presence of mine enemies; thou anointest my head with oil; my cup runneth over. Surely goodness and mercy shall follow me all the days of my life; and I will dwell in the house of the Lord forever.

God always shows up when I least expect it. He provides me with his holy word and loves me. I will praise him always! I am filled with his Holy Spirit. I can't thank him enough. Just as I began to doubt this book and it's purpose he stepped in and confirmed I am truly on the right path. This book is from God through me! I feel it through my very soul. God will allow me to be a witness to the glory of his love for someone out there who is hurting and has been abused. God will use me to bless someone whos heart is so badly scared and feels there is no hope. Many times I have been scared and alone. I learned I do not ever have to be alone! I obey you Lord! Fill me up. Cause my words to flow like a mighty river rushes to the sea! Use me Lord. I ask that you use this vessel of mine to reach out to others. Oh God how I praise you. I love you so much. Thank you for giving me your heart, so mine can beat with pure joy once again! I will shout glory, glory, hallelujah!

God gave me Psalms 37: 34, Don't be impatient for the Lord to act! Keep traveling steadily along his path- way and in due season he will honor you with every blessing, and you will see the wicked destroyed.

The Pain of Hunger and Rejection

There were many trials for me to bear during my high school years. Our family did not have enough money to feed us most of the time. Getting the new clothes a teenage girl wants so badly was just simply out of the question. There were many days I left for school without breakfast only to have to miss lunch as well! My friend Sheryl shared her lunch with me some days, and there were times she would buy it for me. I became very good at just saying I wasn't hungry when another student would ask me why I wasn't eating. Until my senior year there was no free lunch program. If you didn't have money you just did not eat. There were many days I watched fellow students pick at their food and throw a lot of it away. It was so hard to sit there, smell the food, and then watch as they just picked at it and threw most of it in the trash. I was so hungry and to watch untouched food go into the trash was miserable. I never allowed it to show. I never wanted anyone to know how ashamed I was that we had so little at home. Teenagers can be so cruel at times, but I never thought teachers could be as well.

I found out the hard way. I decided to try out for cheerleading my freshman year. I worked every day with my friend Sheryl. We learned all the jumps and cheers we had been given. The day of the trials I was ready. My turn came and I completed all the cheers and completed all the jumps as required. I had such a desire to be accepted by my peers. I was looking for love and friendship. I was devastated when I did not get the cheerleading spot. I ask myself why over and over. But those truths were never revealed to you. The next day I was met by our band teacher. He told me he wanted me to be one of the new majorettes. I was thrilled but I had not even considered it before. I told him I didn't think I could afford to be a majorette or by the required equipment. I had never used a baton. The teacher told me not to worry about a thing he had already arranged everything. He had even made arrangements for training on the use of the baton. He told me I was to see a locally know uniform maker. He had already called and told her what I needed. I told him I would talk with my parents. The next day I started the training. I still wondered why he had done this for me. Almost ten years after I graduated from high school one of the teachers told me the try outs were only a show. The cheerleaders had already been chosen by the coach! I had my answer. It was an answer that just confirmed what I had thought all those years. The band teacher was upset at what they had done to me. He had watched me work so hard every day to be the best! Then to see me cheated out of it even before I showed what I could do was just wrong in his eyes. It was a small town and there were very few who had enough money to afford the required uniforms and camps. We had no money and everyone knew it.

During high school I joined every group I could. I was in the Pep Club, Bible Study class, the Youth Group at my church, I sang in the school chorus, played in the band, Spanish club, majorette, and so many others. I volunteered at the local hospital and was in the local 4-H. I wanted to be accepted; to fit in. Even to this day if you look back at our year book you will not see my picture as one of the majorettes that year. The pictures had already been taken and they would not place mine in the yearbook! Once again I was cheated. I was looking for love and acceptance from people who would never love me back! I just couldn't wrap my mind around how people can be that way and look at themselves in the mirror every day. God has his own way of molding our lives. Even then I couldn't understand that Gods love was all I would ever need.

God gave me Luke 6: 20 – 23 Then he turned to his disciples and said "What happiness there is for you who are poor, for the Kingdome of God is yours! What happiness there is for you who are now hungry; for you are going to be satisfied! What happiness there is for you who weep, for the time will come when you shall laugh for joy! What happiness for you when others hate you and exclude you and insult you and smear your name because you are mine! When that happens, you are mine! When that happens rejoice! Yes leap for joy! For you will have a great reward in awaiting you in heaven and you will be in good company — the ancient prophets were treated that way to. "

My Addiction Revealed

When I was in high school I went to church every Sunday, and was a member of the Youth Group. I came to church as often as I could! As I look back even then I was desperate for love! I was told all the time that Jesus loved me and I believed it. In my heart I knew it, but I needed I wanted, I craved the attention from my family, friends and peers. I volunteered for everything. I was right there when any help was needed. It felt good to serve others. While I was in the moment of helping others I was happy and felt special. Someone needed me. The trouble with that was the task left me feeling cold and empty afterwards. Funny thing, I still feel that way! It is difficult to just help others and not want the quick fix, that feeling of happiness I get from helping someone. The Lord just this very moment spoke to me! He said, "Cheryl, you are a helper junkie!" You get high from helping others. It is like a drug. I feel so joyful and happy when I am helping others, but like a drug I crash and burn once it is over. I am sad and feel so empty. I am exhausted. Why doesn't anyone love me back? I have been given the ability to listen to others and can pick up on the things that make them happy. If they love to get flowers, cards, a box of chocolates, homemade carrot cake or pies, a special soup, or a certain book I am on a mission. I get the things that will make them happy and light up their face. I love to surprise people. They are astonished that I even knew what they like let alone go and get it for them. The joy on their face makes me happy, and I am happy to do it for them! Then later when my birthday, Christmas, or whatever holiday comes around I find there are very few who take the time to do things for me. Did I touch on a nerve? I am flesh and blood, and I too need to feel like someone thinks about me. I have felt many times as though no one feels I deserve to feel special or shown love. Why is it that way? Am I so unworthy? I know now those thoughts were placed in my mind by Satan himself. He has tourchered me all my life with fear and doubts about my worth. Well Satan I am done with you!!!! Jesus is all I need! He will fill me up with his gifts of Mercy, Love, Grace, Salvation, and the precious Blood of Christ and that is all I will ever need! All I had to do was just place him in the front of my life and I will hear him loud and clear! I will receive all the gifts I will ever need. I have been looking for love in all the wrong places, faces and people all my life! God is love!

You Are Not Good Enough for College

I graduated from high school in 1974. I was not the best student. I had average grades, but big plans. I already knew I wanted to become a nurse. I wanted to get married and have four children. My thought was this. I would become a nurse, get married and have children, but my husband would support us. Nursing was the backup plan. You know just in case my husband needed help once in a while. I took college prep classes so I would be ready for the entrance tests. I went to the high school guidance counselor to help me prepare for nursing. I needed to know what courses I would need to get me there. That man proceeded to tell me I wouldn't make it. I was not smart enough. My grades were average and I was not doing that great in math and sciences. He succeeded in making me angry! He also hurt me deeply. I went on to tell my pastor and my parents what the counselor had said. I was encouraged to apply to college anyway. I prayed for God to see me through. As always money was an issue. I needed money to turn in the applications and take all the tests to qualify to apply to the college of nursing. I needed a car and gas money to drive the 60 plus miles a day. I needed books and uniforms. I did not allow that to deter me. I applied anyway! There were only 32 spaces for the fall nursing program. I was able to take all the entrance exams.

About 2 weeks later I was called and ask to come to nursing director's office. I was so nervous. I had no idea what they wanted. Once there I was told I did not do well on the math tests. Math has always been very difficult for me. At that time I was also told there were over 100 applications for the 32 positions. It did not look good for me. I told the nurse thanks and drove home. I prayed that God would hear my prayer and let me through as one of the 32. The doubts rolled in, but God rolled right over them! Praise God!

Bowen Home

My Journey From Home

I had family that lived in a local city. My aunt and uncle came to our house and took me home with them. I needed a job and there were none to be had where I lived. The first job I got after graduation was with mom. We worked in a small factory. Our job was to pull the complete insides out of chickens after they were killed. The chickens flew at us while hanging by their necks on a cable. It was the worst thing I have ever had to do. We literally had to run our hands up inside the chicken and pull out all the organs and do it all at one swoop! You have no idea how hard that is! Those organs are made to stay there! By the end of the day my right hand was so swollen and I could hardly move it. I made a dollar and hour. I worked just one day. Mom and I never went back there. I was so thankful to my aunt and uncle. I was out of that holler and would be given a chance to get a decent job. Maybe I would make it to college after all. Two of my uncles worked at the local paper mill, so they were going to try to get me a job. There were only three summer jobs to be had. There were once again hundreds of applicants. I applied for the job. I prayed to God for that job. I would be able to make and save enough money to buy a car if I got the job. A few days later I was called for the interview. Once the interview was over the man told me I would be better of going to the local hospital and try to get a job since I was trying to become a nurse anyway. I told him I would see him again! I had it on good authority that I was to have one of the three jobs. God was in control! A week later I was called and I had gotten the job. My summer was spent working harder than I could have imagined. I pushed around 50 to 500 pound rolls of paper. I sprayed glue on covers and placed them on the outside edges. The rolls were then placed inside a hot device that sealed the glue. The factory was hot and a fan was all we had to cool us. It was not enough! My shift changed every week. One week I worked first shift then it went to third shift, and then to second shift. My body could never a just to it. I was so happy to be there I did not care. I walked to and from work every day from my aunt and uncles home.

About four weeks into the job I received a letter from the college, and I had made it. I was one of the 32 chosen to become an LPN. Once again God was there for me. He placed people in my life that cared enough about me to go the extra mile and support me. Each of them saw I was willing to do the work. I had taken a leap of faith when all were against me. I applied even when I had been told I was not smart enough to become a nurse. I applied when I had no idea how I would get there or pay for it. God cleared the path for me. I had met him half way. I wanted something badly, and I believed he would see me through, so I put into place the plan and started the journey even knowing it would be difficult. I began a journey knowing it may not come to pass, but I had Jesus as my guide! I worked harder that summer than any other time in my life! I put every penny I could into a savings account. I applied for grants and loans because I still had no idea how I was going to pay for college and I still needed a car to get there. Once again God showed up! I came home one day from work, and wen I got to my Aunts house I noticed what I thought was the ugliest army green Plymouth Valiant I had ever seen parked just outside. I didn't give it any other thought. I walked inside and was greeted by my Aunt Barbara with a big smile. Aunt Barb as I call her said, "You had visitors today." Really, who was it?" I ask. I thought at that time my friends had come and I had missed them. I was disappointed. Aunt Barb stood there with a funny little smile on her face. I looked at her and then ask, Is something wrong? She pulled a set of keys out of her pocket, and dangled them in front of me. Did you happen to notice the green car outside on the street? She tossed me the keys. I looked at them in disbelief. Had my aunt and uncle bought me a car? These are the keys to your new car! What, Where I shouted! I was so excited

I could hardly keep still. Where is it! She opened the front door of the house and pointed to the little green car parked on the street. It was the car I had just thought was the ugliest thing I had ever seen. That car transformed right before my eyes! It was mine and now it was the most beautiful gift I had ever been given! I ran out to the car and my aunt followed right behind me. I now had tears running down my face. God had once again provided for me. I ask my aunt, "Where did it come from?" She laughed and said your mom and dad. What? How? We were so poor how had they done such an awesome thing for me? Where had the money come from? There were a million questions racing through my mind! I gathered my things and drove to mom and dads'. I was sad they had not been able to see the reaction on my face when I received the wonderful gift they had provided for me. I had to tell them thanks and hug them. I found out my dad had sold 4 acres of our land so he could buy a car for my mother and I. Dad and mom saw I was working hard and had been accepted into the nursing program so they made a major sacrifice. I was thrilled. That was the first time I could actually see my dad was proud of me. I had put my faith in God and stepped out on that faith. God had answered my prayers. I was chosen out of over 100 applicants to the nursing program that only had 32 positions. I was chosen for a high paying summer job that also had over 100 applicants for just 3 positions. In the coming months I received grants and enough money to pay for college. The money I had saved that summer gave me the gas money I needed. I was a blessed young woman on her way to completing her dreams. I was on top of the world. Praise God! I learned that summer if you work hard and show appreciation for what you have those around you will reach out and help you achieve your goals. God is in the details but you must be willing to put him in the driver's seat!

Donald L. and Cheryl Bowen-Johnson

Forbidden Love

During that summer at the paper mill I had the pleasure of meeting a lot of new people. I loved to learn new things. I have always been curious. At this plant there were many large machines. Machines that chopped and chipped wood, cooked the wood and turned it into pulp that later transformed it into paper of all sizes shapes and colors. The department where I worked transformed large rolls of paper rolls into packages to be shipped out. My job was to roll the large paper rolls into a single row, spray glue onto paper sleeves and put them on the outside of each roll. I then had to push a button, and a large arm pushed them together to form a heated seal of the glue. Once that was completed the device popped the rolls of paper out and it was placed onto a truck for transportation to it's destination. It was a very hard hot job that I was so thankful for.

On one of those very hot summer days I took my break and walked to water fountain. It was really just an old sink we could wash our hands in. It was so hot that day and the fan just didn't offer much relief. I poured a cup of water and drank it. It was cool and refreshing as I devoured it. I was only 18 at this time. I had really long dark thick hair. I had to have the hair rolled up and out of the way of the machines. It felt heavy and wet from all the sweat. On this day I took down my hair. As I pulled out the bobby pens the hair began to fall covering my back. I bent my head over and swung my hair loose. It felt good to get air to flow through that thick hair. I then splashed the cold water all over my face and arms. When I had finished splashing my face with the water I looked over to see this man just standing there. He had this big beautiful smile on his face. His eyes were the biggest brown eyes I had ever seen. Once our eyes met we just stood there at first. I was shy so I looked away. I had seen this man come and go before, but I was always busy so there was never any conversation, and there was none that day either. I pinned my hair up again and went back to work. During the next week I saw him there more and more. He always smiled and went on his way. I also saw the men I worked with start to tease him. They would make comments like, Hey Don, "What are you doing down here again? We never used to see you so much.", and then they would laugh. All I knew was he was so handsome. One day I was talking with one of the men and was asking about the equipment. During the conversation the man looked at me and smiled. His name is Donald Johnson. It came out of the blue, so I said, "What, Who's name is Donald Johnson?" Then I felt my face begin to turn red and burn hot! They all knew! I had a crush on this man, and I found out he had one for me as well. I began to ask all kinds of questions. Is he married or does he have a girlfriend? I wanted to know everything about him. After that Don began talking to me. He gave me his phone number and we agreed to talk. That evening he called me. We talked for over four hours on that first call. It was as if we had known each other all our lives. We set a date for the weekend. There was to be a popular new Motown group at the fair grounds that weekend. I was so excited! It was the first date and I had never been to a concert like that before. Our time was so easy together. We fit like a hand and glove. He had the sweetest manner about him. He was a gentleman. His voice was deep and sexy. I loved his voice. We fell in love. Donald was already in his early 30's and I was just 18. There was also another division. Donald was African American and I white. It was not a good time to be mixing races. Interracial relationships were highly frowned upon especially in our area. I did not care. I didn't ever see color when I was with him. I was in love with this man. Our time together was relaxed and easy. Don had many friends in town and was involved in many political groups. He was active in the community. He was educated and he had been in the Vietnam War. I had never met anyone who was so educated and had as beautiful a spirit as his was. I was very aware of the people around me. I knew how they felt but I did not care! It made no difference to me. I would not stop seeing this man.

In the beginning of our relationship I was very selective about those I chose to allow in our world. My best friend Sheryl and her husband Gary, my brother Boyd, and my friend Linda. We dated together and spent weekends together. We spent time with friends of Don's. They all loved Don but also knew the road I had chosen would be a difficult one. That did not stop Don and I from being together. My world had changed forever. We dated all through the year of 1974 throughout 1975 while I completed my nursing classes. During that first year there were many times when I would go to my car in the mornings I would find flowers and cards. Don always gave me gifts like that. I fell madly in love and our racial differences didn't matter. There was a path I was on that I knew was against God's law. I was now having a sexual relationship outside of marriage. I knew it was wrong from the very beginning, but I did it anyway. Don and I had been intimate for almost a year. Just before I graduated from college I started to have severe nausea and vomiting. I was so sick I could hardly function. I went to the doctor who told me I may have had a problem with my gallbladder. I went through many tests that all came back ok. At first I did not even think I may be pregnant. Finally I faced up to the fact that I may be. I took a blood test, and sure enough I was pregnant. My world was rocked!! What would I do? What would people think of me. I was not married and the baby's father was a black man. I was a Christian and I had sinned a great sin. I was scared to death! That was not part of my plans. I wanted babies but not outside of marriage. I had walked away from God. He was no longer number one in my life. My pregnancy was difficult to say the least. There were times I was driving to school and had to pull off the side of the road to throw up. Some days I didn't make it. I lost over 20 pounds in the first trimester. My parents began to worry about me. They never dreamed I might be pregnant. I lied to them. My dad wanted to know why I wasn't going to the doctor. I told him I had and was told I may have an ulcer from all the stress of school and so on. It was the hardest thing I had ever done. I looked my father in the eyes and lied to him.

I had stepped away from God and my world was changing faster than I could imagine. I was also deeply in love and now I was alone and pregnant. The man I loved would not be accepted by my family and I knew it. I had to hide the man I loved. How would I ever tell my parents?

I graduated from college and took a job at the local hospital. My father was in and out of the hospital. His heart was failing him. After one of his last stays in the hospital I returned home from work and my mother met me at the door. I didn't know it but my Aunt Gladys had told my mother about Don and that I was pregnant. I had confided in her, and she had told mom. My mother told me she knew everything and that I had to tell my dad before someone else did. I was terrified! I went to my room and packed my things. I knew this would not be a good day. Dad came in and sat down at the kitchen table. I was sitting in the rocking chair in the living room. I told dad I needed to tell him something. I paused and then let it all out. Dad just sat there for a while. He held a cigarette in one hand and a cup of coffee sat on the yellow table before him. Time seemed to stand still and the room got cold. Dad turned and looked at me. For the first time in my life I saw my father with tears running down his face. He told me he could never accept my child and told me he never wanted to see the baby. He ask me if I loved this man and I told him yes. He said well that's good because you just lost a father. He then ask me to leave. I finished putting my things in the back of my car. Just before I left I went back into the house to tell mom goodbye. My dad stood up and hugged me. He cried like a baby but at the same time he told me for your sake I hope you lose the baby or it is born dead. He also told me he hoped I did not marry Don and if I did he never wanted to meet him. I was devastated. I stepped away from dad and said, Dad you always taught us to treat everyone the same, and that in life we have to live in the bed we chose to make. Well dad I plan to live in this bed for the rest of my life. I am sorry you feel like you do, but it will not change my mind. Even though I knew he would react badly it hurt more than I could have imagined. I walked to my car and drove out of that holler. I drove to my best friend's house and called Don. I told him our secret was out and that I was now his. Don told me he loved me and everything would be OK and was glad my parent finally knew, and that he would make arrangements for a place to live. Don already had a house in the area where he lived so I just assumed we would be living there. I stayed at my friend's house. Don called me every day. Then he called me on a Saturday and told me he had rented us an apartment located in Columbus, OH. Don had quit his job at the paper mill and would find a job in Columbus. We both had to make major changes in our lives. I gave up my job and moved away from everything had known.

There were so many against Don and I. So I went to see my pastor. I ask him to show me anywhere in the Bible it said I was never to marry outside of my race. The pastor told me there is no place in the Bible that says there is a law from God that Don and I should not be together. I was told that society made up the rule. With the information I walked away happy. I now knew God was not against Don and I. I did know I was wrong in having a sexual relationship with Don out of marriage.

Don and I moved to Columbus, OH in the summer of 1975. I was happier than I had ever been in my life. Don and I moved into a little two bedroom apartment and settled in. For the first time I had a home of my own. It was clean and had a lot of closet space. There was a bathroom and running water. I had a man who loved me and assured me we would be OK. I was safe and our baby would have her own room.

It was also a very scary time for me. I had left my whole way of life. I was unable to see my mom and family and friends. My father refused to allow my mother to see or to help me. I was on my own and pregnant for the first time. Even though I had gone against what I knew was God's law I knew he still loved me. I moved from a small home located in an area called Owl Creek. I was a small town country girl who had grown up in a holler. I knew nothing of the city life. Yet here I was in one of the largest cities in the state, and I was alone most of the time while Don worked. I was not used to all the city lights and large shopping malls. I was used to only the faces of family and church members. Here I was exposed to a multitude of different people and places. It was thrilling but also very scary. There was no one to call just to talk to because it was long distance and we couldn't afford the calls.

I began to decorate our tiny apartment. We did not have much, but I was so happy with what we had. Don spent long hours at his new job. I didn't know my way around this big new city, so I was afraid to go out and explore. I waited until Don came home, or we completed shopping on the weekends.

Donald finally took me to meet his family. His sister Joanne was one of the sweetest lady I had ever met. Joanne welcomed me to her home like she had always known me. My first visit to her home she took me into her kitchen and had me peel potatoes while she fried chicken. Joanne is to this day one of the best cooks I have had the pleasure to know! Joanne has a heart of gold and a heart for God! Joanne is the closest thing to an angel here on earth I will ever have the pleasure to meet.

I missed my church and all my friends and siblings. I missed my mom and dad. I missed home! I had so many questions about the baby growing inside me. I knew it was going to be a girl and already had her named. I wondered what she would be like. What will she look like? I couldn't wait to meet her. I named her Christina Marie Johnson long before she came screaming into this world. I wanted to be the best mother in the world. I chose not to work until after she was born, so that put a financial strain on us, but I was so used to being poor it didn't matter to me. Looking back I know I chose not to work because I was scared and insecure. I had no idea where to go or how to get there. After a few months Don lost his job, so he started his own Home Insulation Business. Don came home less and less. Don worked long hours and even on weekends to fit the jobs into the people's schedules. I began to meet people that lived around the apartment complex. It felt good to have people to talk to again. The relationship I made there are still friends today. We spent hours setting outside on the steps and talking. We shared music and laughter. I needed that so badly. These new friends didn't care that I was unmarried and that Don was African American. It became easier to live there. I was making this strange place my home.

My doctor was located an hour south of Columbus. When I had an appointment with the GYN I took the time to go and visit my mother where she worked. I took mom yellow roses and candy. I wanted her to feel special. It was always such a treat to see her smile when I surprised her. Dad couldn't stop me from going there. It took months for me to make the first trip back to holler. I was as stubborn as my father.

Bowen's Road

Returning Home

I was about six months pregnant when I first went back. I made sure I had new clothes on, and I drove the new car. I stopped at the local stores on my way home and purchased some groceries. I knew there was still very little there to eat. I bought all kinds of lunch meats, breads, milk, candy, sodas, and assorted chips. This was the first trip back since dad had told me to leave, so I had no idea how he would respond to this visit. I was scared and had no idea how he would receive me. I needed him to know I was OK and doing very well. Even more I wanted dad to see how well I was, and that Don was really taking care of me. As soon as my brothers and sisters saw me coming they ran to the car to greet me. After the hugs and kisses I went to the back of the car and opened the trunk. They were so excited to see all those bags. I had them carry the groceries into the house. Dad was sitting at the head of the little yellow table located in our tiny kitchen when I walked in. He had that cigarette in his hand and a cup of coffee sitting in front of him as usual. He looked at me and said hello. He ask me how I was doing. We had very polite conversation. The kids were standing all around the table and tore open all the bags of food and started to make sandwiches and open sodas and candy. The bags of chips were torn open and the feasting began. I was so happy to see them. I was happy to see them eating and having fun. That visit went much better than I expected but it was still very clear dad was not ever going to except my decision. Dad told me I was welcome to come home to visit, but I could never bring my baby home and he did not want to ever meet Don. His ways were set in stone! I made several trips home after that and brought gifts and food.

My mother worked in a local nursing home and there was where I visited her. I always made sure I had gifts in hand on each visit to see her. I wanted everyone there to know how much my mother meant to me. She worked so very hard as a cook there. Everyone loved her pies! She was the best cook. My mother could cook well and would try any new recipe she could locate. Mom was famous throughout our family for her chicken and noodles. They were expected at each family gathering. Dad would not allow my mother to call or come to see me. My mother and I were more like friends than mother and daughter. The loss of her in my life was more painful than I could ever imagine. As bad as I felt; I can not begin to know how it must have been for her. She was not to be allowed in her oldest daughter's life, or share in the birth of her first grandchild.

The Birth of My Beautiful Christina

Christina Marie came to me and her father on April 11, 1976. She weighed 9 pounds and 1 ounce and was 21 inches long. The birth of my daughter was not easy! Don and I had spent the weekend at our friend's home. It was on Sunday morning. During the night labor had begun, but I did not realize what was taking place. I was up and down all during the night. I felt like I had to go to the bathroom about every 10 minutes, then it went to every 5 minutes. The pain became worse as the time passed. Finally around 8 AM I realized what was happening to me. I went to the bedroom and woke up Don. I told him I was in labor. By this time I was having contractions every 2 to 3 minutes and they were so painful I could barely stand. I woke up Sheryl and we started to the hospital. I remember thinking we were never going to make it there. I was going to have this baby in the back seat of the car. The pain was so terrifying. In all my life I had never felt anything like this. Once we reached the hospital I tried to walk down the hallway to the labor and delivery room. I would stop and double over in pain. I wanted my mommy! I was like a little girl and she was the only person who could help me. I begged my friend to call her and tell her to come to me! I was scared to death! As a nurse I knew what was happening and had seen many go through this process. I was not prepared for this agony. My mother was called, but dad would not let her come to me.

In the 70's a woman was placed in a hospital labor room alone. She was not allowed to have her husband or family support team in the room. It was a time of pain and suffering the mother endured with strangers. Mothers were given medication to help with the pain. The medication for the most part wiped out most of the memory of the pain. Fortunately for me I knew one of the nurses at the hospital. She had been a friend of Dons before we met. I recall the doctor coming in and out of the room. I remember the pain of the rectal exams he performed. I didn't understand why he did them. Something was wrong and I knew it, but I could not ask questions. The medication had me so dazed I couldn't function. The pain went on for what seemed to me to be an eternity. I was also beginning to see the worry on the doctors and nurses faces as they encourage me. After several exams and hours of contractions that came in painful waves every 1 to 2 minutes it was decided I should have an x-ray. They took me out into the hallway and allowed me to see and talk to Don and Sheryl. It was only a short hello but it was good for me to see their faces. It was then I learned I was not to see my mother. I do not remember the x-ray, but I do remember a nurse laying across my abdomen and yelling for me to push. I didn't know until the next day what had happened to us. Christina was too big for my pelvic to allow her to pass through, so they used forceps and had to surgical cut my vaginal wall in 3 places. I should have had a C-section but it was too late to perform. Christina was literally pushed and pulled into this world. She suffered a broken collar bone and had large bruises on both sides of her face. Her little head was shaped like a cone. Not only was I cut in 3 places I had also been torn. I was given what they called a Saddle block before delivery, so now I was to lay flat on my back. Christina was not brought to me until the next day. I was still in so much pain and now I had a severe headache. The first time my baby girl was brought into my room the nurse placed her on my chest. At first I thought this can't be right. She seemed to be so big. It felt more like a 3 month old was given to me. I turned her to meet my eyes. When I looked into her eyes I felt the very presence of God. He had saved our lives and there she was my baby girl. I whispered hello Christina. Christina looked at me with the most beautiful big brown eyes I had ever seen. They were like a dark well you could get lost in. She had thick and long dark hair. Her skin was a beautiful milk chocolate color that seemed to be dusted with golden light. She was the most beautiful and precious thing I had ever seen. Her lips were large and perfectly shaped. Her eyes followed me as I talked to her. I was filled with a joy words could not express. Christina was a gift sent to me from God, and a pure bundle of joy. How could anyone look at upon her face and not love her? I wanted my mother to see her so badly. I know had it not been for God's grace and mercy my child and I would have died. I thanked him for that with all my heart!

The Visit

I was always allowed to visit my friend Sheryl and stay with her. Sheryl loved me unconditionally. It was a month after the birth of Christina, and I was tired of being in the apartment, so I drove home for a visit. Once there I called and ask mom if she would come. She told me she would try, but dad would have no part of it. It was good just to hear her voice. Mom arrived and for the first time saw Christina. She fell in love with her. Mom could only stay a short time, but it was so good to spend this time with her.

Thomas Jr. &
Rose Marie Bowen

A Fathers Denial

During this visit mom told me dad was getting worse now. His health was failing fast. He was losing weight because it was very difficult for him to swallow anything. His heart was so large now it began to push against his esophagus. Dad spent more and more time in the local hospital. I always came to see him. He would ask how I was but he never did ask about his granddaughter. I brought her with me at every visit. She was adored by all my family, but dad had too much pride and so did I. I refused to just bring her in to his room. My father had told me he never wanted to see my baby and so he would not! My nephew Joseph was born 2 months after Christina. He was always there to visit dad as well. It was so hard to see my father acknowledge him and never even ask about my baby.

The Loss of My Earthly Father

My father's illness took him from us during the month of October
in 1976. My father passed away never seeing his oldest grandchild.
He never asked about her.

Don and I married August 28, 1976, but dad never had the pleasure
of meeting my husband. Don was always sad about that. Don was
the type of man that everyone loved. He was kind and generous.
He had a way about him that just made you want to know him.
Don used to tell me, If I could just meet him and talk to him I
know I could change his mind. That was never to happen. Don
was well aware that the color of his skin made a lot of people
angry, but that didn't stop him from loving people. That fact
only seemed to make him want to get to know them more. He
wanted to show people he was more than the color on his shin.
He was a loving and gentle man. He chose to love them in spite
of their ugly ways. Don's family told me several times that he was
a true man of God. Don had always loved the Lord and he went
to church on a regular basis.

The Vietnam Conflict

Don was called to serve his country and he did so with pride. But something happened to him while there. His sisters told me Don returned a changed man. Once home again he did not go to church and he would not talk about where he was or about what happened to make the change. Don was no longer filled with the Holy Spirit. The light was gone from his beautiful big brown eyes. He was forever changed. Don became active in the community and served on several political boards.

A Cold Wind

After the birth of our daughter Don began to work harder and harder to support our family. He came home later and later. Things were different now. I began to see a different man. He became distant and withdrawn. There was a cold wind in our house. It was then I began to push for a real home. I wanted out of the apartment. I wanted a back yard for our daughter to play in. We needed more room! We lived on the third floor and it was difficult to pack a baby and all the things that went with her up all those flights of stairs. When I was alone I had to decide where to leave my baby. Did I leave her alone in the care while I carried groceries up all those stairs, or did I leave her alone in the apartment? Don agreed and we began our search for the new home. We spent months looking! The homes we looked at were either too expensive or in the wrong area. One day late in 1977 Don found a house located in the north of Columbus. We bought and moved into the home November 1977. It was perfect timing. I was now pregnant with our son Nathan Lee. It was a little two story two bedroom house with a full basement. The yard was fenced in. I was happy!

The Birth of My Son

Once again God spared the life of me and my child. It was a very difficult pregnancy and labor. After the birth of our son I began to hemorrhage. Just after he was born I saw a frantic look on my doctor's face. The nurse was told to lay my head down and strap my arms to the side of the bed. I began to feel cold. My teeth chattered uncontrollably, and my body shook. I looked at my husband. I felt as if the life was draining out of me. It was; I was bleeding to death. My doctor looked at me and said, Cheryl you are bleeding out, I have to try to stop the bleeding. How I asked? He told me he would have to take his hand and go back inside me and massage the uterus. No I screamed! I was scared. The doctor told me it was the only was he could stop the bleeding. Don took one arm and the nurse took my other one. They held me down while the doctor performed the life saving but painful procedure. Other nurses were rushing all around me hanging bags of blood. I shook so violently it was hard to stay on the bed. I was freezing. I felt life leaving me. God please help me I prayed! Then the pain stopped. I felt the warm blankets being placed over me. The bleeding stopped. Although I saw my son for a fleeting moment he was another beautiful child given to me by Gods grace. My son had been rushed to NICU. It would be a week before I could hold him in my arms. I begged to see and hold him, but was not allowed. I was told we were both just too ill to be together. I carried and low fever and so did Nathan. After several days in the hospital I was sent home alone without my son Nathan. It was 7 days after his birth before he was allowed to come home. Nathan entered into the world on June 27 and came home to us on July 2. God once again showed up and protected us as a family. Nathan was referred to as the beautiful dark red baby by Don's sisters. Nathan had thick long dark brown hair and the biggest brown eyes. They were beautiful. He was the picture of perfection! When he looks into your eyes he fills you up with a smile. Nathan has the same gentle spirit as his father. He is kind to a fault and will help anyone who needs it. He is a beautiful gentle man! I am proud to call him my son! God had blessed me. I now had a son and a daughter, a husband who loved and supported me. I completed the nursing degree I wanted. I had a nice home! With hard work and God's grace I had fulfilled all my dreams. I was a very happy woman. I was blessed!

Don's business began to flourish. We had to hire3 men to help out. Don and I had purchased 6 different pieces of property. I had just been hired as an L.P.N. on a state job with good pay and full medical benefits. We had met a lot of new faces on our street and were making friends. I was introduced to a newly formed group of Christians. This group of people met in an apartment located just across the street from me. They were the closest thing to the church I had grown up in and I was beginning to put God first in my life again. That small group is now in charge of one of the largest churches located in Columbus, OH. The Vineyard located on Cooper Road. I was home! OH how our world was about to change!

Dolly and Thunderbolt

We Are Blessed to Achieve Our Goals but We Are not Always Allowed to Keep Them

It was early one summer morning. Don and I were sitting on the side of the bed talking and planning our weekend. Don stood up in front of the window and picked up his shirt. He reached his arms up to pull the shirt over his head. It was then I saw it. There was a lump about the size of a walnut under his left arm pit. I reached out to touch it. At first Don jumped. He thought I was going to tickle him. I told him what I saw. Then as I examined it I ask how long it had been there? My first thought was Cancer! I did not speak those words out loud. Don then told me it had been there for a while but he didn't think it was any big deal. Meantime my mind was reeling. Please God do not let this be cancer.

Monday arrived and I called my friend and co-worked to get the name of a good doctor. I called and made the appointment for Don. On the first visit he was examined and told they didn't think it was more than a swollen lymph gland, but told Don he would need to return for a biopsy. Don of course did not reschedule the appointment. A month or so later I started to see changes in him. He was losing weight and having night sweats. Don would literally soak the bed at night. He started to have high temperatures. One morning I walked into the bathroom and there stood my beautiful husband. He was a shell of a man. All he had on were his undershorts. He was so thin I could count each one of his ribs, and his feet and legs were so swollen he barely walk. The tears ran down my face. Don, why didn't you tell me. Why had I not seen it? Don was so sick but he got up every morning before I did and went to work. He came home late at night. I went straight to the phone and called the doctor. I scheduled an appointment for the very next day. A multitude of blood tests were competed and x-rays done. Don was scheduled to have a biopsy. Don never talked about any of this and I was scared to death. I prayed that God would save us!

Don was admitted to the hospital and the biopsy was done. Once he returned to his room I sat there beside him while he slept. It was now late in the evening. I was sitting there praying to God to help us. The room was dark except for the city lights streaming into the room. I sat there beside Don and listened to him breathing. This was the man I was supposed to live with the rest of my life.

Don was still sleeping and I had almost fallen asleep when two doctors walked into the room. They did not wake Don. The doctors introduced themselves as the oncologist who would be taking care of Don. "Oncologist!" I screamed inside! My husband had cancer! I took a deep breath. The doctor did not appear to notice he had just kicked me in the stomach! Before they even said the word Cancer I knew! Once they knew I was his wife they told me what I feared the most. Don has cancer. We are not sure what type it is, but we are sure it is a Lymphoma type. The biopsy sample has been sent away and it will take about 3 weeks for the results to come back. He was so matter of fact about it! I sat there stunned! Are you absolutely sure? The reply was yes we are. I was stunned! I was scared! The doctor told me to call if I had any questions. What? Was he crazy? I had so many questions I couldn't get them out. I had questions about my questions! I had no idea what we were dealing with or what type of treatment he would require. Would my beautiful husband live or die. Was the cancer treatable? The doctors left the room. I was in a state of shock and I had no one to lean on! I can't lose my husband!

I pulled myself together and prepared to leave the room. I still had to pick up the kids. Don was still sleeping and I didn't want to wake him. I leaned over and gave him a kiss on the cheek. He looked so very peaceful there in that moment. He looked up at me. I told him I was going to get the kids and would be back in the morning. Get some sleep baby. I left the room. As I walked to my car I began to fall apart. The tears flowed like running water. I picked up the kids and drove home. It was not a restful sleep for me.

The next morning Don told me to come and get him. He was being released. The plan of care could not start until we identified the type of cancer he had. We went home and tried to resume our lives. It was so hard to watch the beautiful man I married suffer in such a way and I could do nothing for him. Don wanted to and tried to continue to work. He could not! The fevers and night sweats became worse. He lost more and more weight. He became so weak it was difficult for him to complete even small tasks like brushing his teeth. My husband was losing hope.

About three weeks went by and I received a call from the oncologist. He wanted me to come into the office for a consultation. Don was already back in the hospital He had become so weak and had developed shingles all over his abdomen and around to his back. He was now in lots of pain as well. He was also receiving blood transfusions. I called a friend and ask her to go with me to the appointment. Once I arrived for the appointment I was sent into the doctor's office and ask to wait. I sat there waiting while the doctor finished with another patient. It was only about 15 minutes, but it was like an eternity to me. I tapped my nails against the table and my feet bounced in unison. I was so nervous! Finally the doctor entered into the room. He sat down at the desk in front of me. He picked up a folder and opened it. He studied it for a moment, and then looked up at me. Then those words came pouring out. You husband, Don, has stage four Non-Hodgkin's Lymphoma. Once again the tears came flowing. "What does that mean,?" I asked. Where do we go from here? What do we do? How long does he have? Is it treatable? The doctor told me as gently as he could that my husband may only have 3 months to live. What did you say? I asked him to repeat what I had already heard. He repeated it again, and then said, "There is no cure, and the treatment itself can be deadly." Don's immune system is already so compromised. Then I asked, "Does Don know yet?" The doctor told me no, he had not told Don yet, but he would be there this evening to the hospital to talk with him. My world began to fall apart! I cried so hard I could barely breathe. This can't be true. This had to be some kind of a night

73

mare! God why are you doing this to us? My friend tried her best to comfort me but it was no use. I took a few minutes and then pulled myself together. I needed to make calls and get ready to go to the hospital. I needed to be there for Don. I needed him desperately. I needed my mother and my siblings around me.

I called mom and told her. She told me they were on their way and would be there in about an hour or so. I picked up the kids and told Don's sister Joanne. I drove to the hospital. Some of the family started to arrive, but I met them in the family area. I didn't want anyone to disturb Don until after he saw the doctor.

The Message

The oncologist arrived and came into the room with us. He then ask if we would mind meeting him in the family area just down the hall. It was private. Don had a roommate and the doctor didn't want to give Don his diagnosis in front of anyone! We all gathered there in that little room. The doctor delivered the news. Don, he said, "The test results have been returned and you have Stage 4 Non-Hodgkin's Lymphoma." I am sorry to be the one to have to give this information. There is no known cure at this time for this form of cancer, and at this stage you may only make it 3 months. Dead silence filled the room. Don sat there for a while looking away from us. When he looked up his eyes were full of tears. Are you sure doctor? The doctor then told Don, we don't know exactly the amount of time for sure, but your symptoms are so severe at this time and your immune system is shot! You will require blood transfusions and packed platelets and a lot of really dangerous Chemotherapy treatments that will make it even worse. The side effects from the chemotherapy will cause severe drops in platelets and all other cells. The treatment to kill the cancer cells also destroys the good cells. You will need to be in the hospital for weeks at a time, and there will be days you can not see your family. You will have severe nausea and vomiting and elevated temperatures. It is up to you to choose what you want to do. Think it over and lets us know. The doctor excused himself and left the area. I sat there. What do you say to someone you love that has just been given a death sentence? I sat down beside him and we just held on to each other and cried. That was Feb. of 1979. Don was released to go home until the plan of care was established.

The Therapy Began

Don and I tried to pick up the pieces and live as normally as we could. I went back to work. Don started the Chemotherapy. He was in and out of the hospital. Sometimes he spent weeks there. The drugs stripped most of the red blood cells and destroyed most of his platelets. He developed temperatures of 106 and had hallucinations. He got so bad sometimes he was placed in isolation to protect him. The kids were not allowed to come to see him. I was the only one allowed most of the time. I saw what was once a beautiful healthy and vibrant man wither away right before my eyes. The very color of his skin changed. What was once vibrant and beautiful dark skin was now dull and dark. He had dark circles around his eyes and looked so helpless. The vomiting was so bad he couldn't eat or drink, so he had IV's that filled him up with fluids. I left that hospital many many days crying so hard I could barely walk. Don and I prayed that he would be healed. The weeks flowed into months. Don was approached to try a new type of treatment. There are no guarantees that they would work, but maybe there would be more time. He agreed to the experimental chemotherapy treatments. It was a very difficult treatment. Don lost all his hair and a lot more weight. But after a few months he began to feel better. He put on weight and his hair grew back. He got to where he looked healthy again. The hospital staff became like a second family during this period in our lives.

My days were filled to the breaking point. I was just 24 years old. I had a husband who was in and out of the hospital, a full time job I had to keep because we depended on the insurance and the money. I had two beautiful babies that depended on me. Christina was 3 and Nathan was 1 years old. Many days after I left my job Don would request I cook something special for him and bring it back to the hospital. I wanted to do anything to make him more comfortable. That meant I climbed out of my bed every day at 4:30 am. Dressed the two babies and myself, I drove from the North side of town to take them to their aunts. She lived all the way across town to the east side. I then had to drive back to the west side of town to my job that started at 6AM. I worked an 8 hour shift and then made the round trip again to pick up the kids. If Don wanted something special I had to drive home cook and then go back downtown to the hospital to deliver the food to him. After all that most of the time he was just too sick to eat it. I loved this man and I would have done anything to make him feel more comfortable. This schedule began to take it's toll on us both! The norm was now working, hospital, shuffling the children from aunt to aunt, moms and sisters, friends and neighbors. It hurt so desperately to see my husband in so much pain and I couldn't change a thing to make it better. Don always held his head up high and was loved by everyone on the oncology unit. He had a smile and a laugh that lit up the darkest room! He was so exceptional and so gracious the nurses started to put him in with the patients that had lost all hope. He was dying and yet he made others feel better. He was loved by all, and yet I began to feel like he didn't need me anymore. He slowly pushed me aside. He would call and ask me not to come to the hospital. He would tell me I needed to take the babies home and get some rest. He didn't communicate to me much anymore. At first I will admit it was somewhat of a relief. I was tired and I did need to rest and spend time at home with the kids. The house had fallen apart and needed to be cleaned badly. We talked every day, but the visits to the hospital became fewer and fewer. It was as though he began to push me away. Looking back I wonder if it was easier not to see me and the kids. We were the reminders of the life he was going to miss. It had to have hurt him so badly. I began to bargain with God, Please God heal him or take him home with you. I don't want him to suffer anymore. Thank God he knew better than I what my husband needed. I was now starting to be angry with God. Why are you doing this to us? We need Don more than you do Lord. We have children that need their daddy. We have a life here. Please don't take him away! Heal him Lord! There were a lot of those conversations with God in that short period of time. It was a very dark time in our lives, but I would soon find out it was to become so much darker.

The Rape

It was not enough that our lives were turned upside down there was even more unspeakable things to come my way! I had visited my husband after work as I often did. On this day he was feeling a little better so we had a great time together. We talked about the day's events and the children. It hurt him not to see them, but it was too risky at this stage of treatment. He had to be kept away from as many outside germs as possible, so the kids were not allowed to visit at this time. I told Don I had left the kids with my supervisor so I couldn't stay as long as I wanted to. It was also during the week and I had to work the next day. So I gathered my purse, and kissed him goodbye. I walked outside and before I got to my car I looked for the keys. I couldn't find them anywhere. While I was standing there on the sidewalk in front of the hospital searching for my keys I happened to see a man standing across the street. I couldn't see his face, but he was well dressed. He had on a white shirt and a nice pair of black slacks. I don't know why he stood out from the crowd but he did. It was a beautiful sunny day, and there were people everywhere. I gave the man no other thought. I went back up to the room and there were my keys lying on the bedside table. Don was scheduled for testing so he was not in the room when I returned. I picked up the keys and made my way back to the car. I was lucky that day I thought because I found a place right in front of the hospital on the street. I didn't have to pay for parking. I walked across the street and headed to my car. I put in the keys and opened the door. Just as I started to get into my car the man I had seen earlier approached me. He held out a pair of sunglasses and ask me if they were mine. Just as I looked up at him to say no he pulled out the gun. He told me to slide over and he got inside the car with me. He pushed the gun into my ribs, and told me to start the car. I was terrified in that moment! I was driving a very large green Chevy Impala at the time. It had a full front seat, so he was able to keep me right beside him with gun pushed into my rib cage at all times. I looked all around me. There were people everywhere. They were walking right by me! I was screaming inside please can't you see what is happening to me! No one noticed. The man drove off. He ask for my name and I gave him my sister Brenda's name. To this day I don't know why I did that. I just didn't want him to know me. If he knew me personally he may be able to get to my family. I would be enough! I told him one of my tail lights were out and that he should be careful driving. Even though I was screaming on the inside somehow I managed to remain calm. I didn't want to upset this man in anyway. After just a short distance he drove to the back of the one of the parking lots. He stopped and turned off the car. He told me to get out and walked me to the back. Funny thing he never ask me for my purse. He told me he needed to use my car but he did not intend to hurt me. And yet the gun remained on me at all times. The man opened the trunk of the car and told me to climb in. I moved around some of the tools and items there and climbed into the trunk of my car. He closed the lid on me. Oh my GOD I could hear in my head. He is going to kill me. A storm of questions began to rise up inside of me. I was so scared. I heard the car engine start and could smell the exhaust fumes from the tailpipe. As he pulled away I thought about my babies and Lillian. I would not be there to get my children. She would be so upset with me. It was the first time she had ever taken care of them and I was not coming back when I told her I would be. My husband was in the hospital dying with little time left to live. OH my God I am never going to see my family again. God Please help me. It was then a calm fell over me. If I was going to die so be it. Jesus was in control. I thought about my purse. It was a curious thing. The man did not even ask to see my purse. I had received my check that day and Don's disability check. I had over $200.00 in cash on me. He didn't see any of it. It was one more miracle. I took my wallet and the checks out of my purse as well as the cash. I tucked them behind the spare tire. If he did ask later to see my purse all would be gone. Even if I did not make it back at least my family would have their money. While I was in the trunk of that car I prayed, "Lord, "If it be your will that on this day I should die I ask that you bless and protect my family. Jesus, Jesus, Jesus, take care of my babies. In Jesus name Amen." I could hear the cars all around me now and the speed of the car accelerated. We were now on the freeway. I had no idea where I was being taken. I held on tightly to the tire and tried not be thrown around in the trunk. It was difficult to breath. The gas fumes were consuming my lungs. I was getting a headache now as well. It seemed like an eternity to me, but we finally came to a stop. I heard the man turn off the engine. I then heard another man's voice. I was now even more terrified. What are they going to do. Every imaginable thought raced through my mind. I then heard the man walking back to the trunk of the car. He put the keys in the lock and the door opened allowing the sun to burst into the dark place. The light hurt my eyes so I covered them with my hands. Once the trunk lid opened he pointed the gun at me and ask me if I was OK? In my head I was screaming, No I am not OK I have been taken at gun point and put in the trunk of my car and forced away from my family. Are you crazy?!! Am I OK?! What kind of man is this? He told me he wanted to check on me and give me some fresh air, but I would have to stay there. The gun was ever present. I was allowed fresh air for only a couple of minutes. He then closed the trunk again putting me into darkness. I was there for several minutes. It felt like an eternity. While he was gone all sorts of things went through my mind. Will he kill me, rape me, or worse. My mind played tricks on me. I thought about screaming, but was afraid the other man was standing guard. Then out of the blue I heard someone running towards the car. I heard the footsteps reach the car. The door opened and the engine started. The car pulled off as fast as he could go. I was thrown all over the back of that trunk. This is it I thought I will not live much longer. Jesus take control! The man drove for a short time and pulled over by the side of the road. He got out and came back to the trunk and opened the lid. He pointed the gun at me and told me to get out. It was difficult. I hurt from being thrown around and my eyes burned. I had a headache. I climbed out of the car. He told me to get in and drive. He slid in the front of the car and while holding the gun in my ribs told me to get in beside him. He was now in the middle of the seat and I was the driver. I wondered what he had just done. Why did he need me and my car? What was he going to do to me? He began talking to me, and then told me what the woman had said when he robbed her. He asks me why I had been to the hospital. I told him I was visiting a friend. I did not want him to know anything personal about me. He then ask me if I had ever wanted to have sex with a black man? I ask him,"What do you mean." He repeated the question. I told him, "No I have not." I was not going to tell him I was married to a beautiful wonderful black man! He laughed and said I bet you have always wanted to. I made a choice not to look this man directly in the face! I looked down or forward. Never directly at him! He had me drive through downtown and over to the East side of Columbus. He had me pull into a dark alley. I knew of the area, but I wasn't exactly sure where I was. Once he had me park the car he told me to get out and come to the passenger side. The gun was ever present. He made me walk around to the passenger side of the car. He told me to take off my clothes. There was a couple standing down the alley, but they never looked our way. He then made me lie down on the front seat. There he lay on top of me and pointed the gun to me temple. He raped me. Once he was done he stood up and told me to get dressed. I pulled on my clothes. Now I was shaking violently and crying. He looked at me and then he had the nerve to ask if I needed any money. I couldn't believe it. You just kidnapped and raped me and you want to know if I need money. I said as calmly as I could, No thank you. If you had to go through all this for money, you need it more than I do. He gave me the keys and walked away. Praise God he gave me back my life!

I ran to the driver side and got in the car. I started the car and took off as fast as I could. I drove until I found a street I was familiar with and drove straight to the hospital where my husband was. I pulled into the ER parking lot and ran into the ER. I lost a shoe; I had grease and dirt all over me. I was now literally falling apart. I ran into the ER and stood at the desk screaming for someone to help me. Help me please I have been raped. People all over the ER were looking at me, and then the doors to the ER swung open and the nurses came running to me. I was taken to a private room. There I was examined and had to relive that nightmare over and over again. I had to talk to the nurse the doctors the police and the detectives. I kept telling them I want to see my husband. They were shocked to find he was a dying patient in this very hospital. I had to wait to see him until I had been examined and gave my report. The man who raped me told me what he had done and what he had said to the person he robbed. I told it to the police and detectives. It was almost an exact report as the lady gave them that had been robbed. I cried for my husband. I was told they had called the nurses on the oncology floor and Don was being brought to me, but I had to be examined first. It was as if I was being raped all over again. Each time I had to repeat it all. It was horrible. I sobbed. I could not stop. I felt betrayed and used. How would my husband see me now? Would he accept me? My mother and family had been called as well as Lillian who had my babies. Lillian brought me the kids and another co-worker came in. I was able to see all of them after all the interviews and exams. I was exhausted!!!! I grabbed onto my friend from work. I latched onto her and could not let go. At the time she didn't know what had happened to me.

Don was brought to me in a wheelchair. He was so sick and weak from the treatment. He got up and pulled me into his arms. He and I cried together. He told me everything was going to be OK and that he loved me! He loved me. He took my face in his hands and repeated I LOVE YOU! Nothing can ever change that. He was my glue. He held me together on that horrible night. He was weak and the nurses made him return to his room. We said our goodbyes and I went to home with my friend. My mom and stepfather took the kids home with them. Mom really wanted me home with her, but I needed to be near Don.

My friend took me home with her. There she ran a hot bath for me and gave me clean clothes to wear. She put me in her bed and took care of me. I stayed with her for the next two weeks. God saved me and put good people in my path to help me heal. That rapist however took away the little trust I had left. The police never caught the rapist even though there were 8 sets of finger prints found on my car. The rapist never did anything to hide the prints on his hands. He did not wear gloves. He was never found.

> *God gave me Galatians' 3: 22-23 "Well then are God's laws and God's promises against each other? Of course not! If we could be saved by his laws, then God would not have had to give us a different way to get out of the grip of sin ------ for the scriptures insist we are all it's prisoners. THE ONLY WAY OUT is through in Jesus Christ, the way of escape open to all who believe him."*

Jesus answered my prayers. Once again he saved me from deaths door. I accepted the horrible event in my life. I took time to rest and then began to resume some sense of normality. After all I had a job to go to, 2 beautiful babies who depended on me and a husband who was very ill. It was difficult to do. I had to return to the place I had been abducted several times a week. That is where my husband was most of the time. I would not go to my car alone anymore. I had to have security walk me to my car. After that attack I was scared to death anytime anyone tried to approach me, and it did not matter if it was a man or woman.

The months flew by us. I was beginning to allow myself to think Don was going to beat this thing. He had been given 3 months upon diagnosis. He had now lived over 17 months. I was grateful to God for everyday I had my husband. He felt so much better we planned and went on a vacation with my sister and her husband to Virginia Beach, Va. It was August 1980. We had a really great time together. Don was weak and thin, but he had a head full of beautiful brown hair again. It was a great time of rest and relaxation.

Once we returned home Don had to go back to the hospital for treatment. We were back to our normal routine again. Don had reactions this time to the therapy. His platelet count and red book cell count plummeted. He was too sick to come home for more than eight hours once a week. On the last visit Don made home I noticed a rather large black mark on the bottom of his left foot. I ask how he had gotten it and he told me he didn't even know it was there. The area was large and black and hard to touch. I told him to make sure he showed it to the doctors and nurse when he got back to the hospital. We spent the rest of our time playing with the kids. Don got down on the floor and let the kids ride on his back. They had a great time that day. Don chose to take a cab that night back to the hospital. I was tired and so were the kids. He didn't want us to have to go out again. Once he was gone I called the nurse and told them what I had found on his foot. They assured me it would be checked out as soon as he got back. I climbed into bed. I had another long day ahead of me.

The Call

I was at work. It was just two days after the visit home. I was sitting across from my supervisor at her desk. The phone rang as it did many times in that nursing office. This was different! I could see the color drain from Lil's face. She looked at me and said it's the hospital. She handed me the phone. I said hello. One of the nurses we had grown so found of was on the end of the line. Cheryl, Don has taken a turn for the worst and you need to get here as soon as possible. She would not tell me anymore. Just get here as soon as you can. I ask the nurse to make sure she told Don I loved him and I was on my way. I was terrified! God please not now! Don't take my husband. I ran to the car and drove as fast as I could. I prayed and begged God all the way there. Please don't take him. I ran as fast as I could to get to him. Once I got to his room it was full of nurses and doctors, machines for x-rays and blood work. I was frantic. Let me in Let me in I cried. I have to see him. They moved and allowed me to get the side of his bed. Don was gasping for air. They were putting tubes everywhere. I realized we had never talked about this moment. We had nothing planned. There was no will and he had not told anyone what he wanted to do in the end. He was so desperate to breath, but too weak to write on the paper he had been given. He tried to talk to me and tried to write to me. He just couldn't so he finally gave up. I told him to relax we would be able to talk later once he was stabilized. I was crying but tried not to let him see it. He looked at me and his eyes were filled with tears. It broke my heart into pieces! I love you Don, I love you baby, it will be

OK. I could not begin to understand what he must have been thinking and feeling in the moment. They rushed Don to the Intensive Care Unit. Oxygen was applied but it was not enough! Don had to be placed a on a ventilator. He was unable to breathe on his own. They worked on him for a long time. Each time he came to he pulled the Vent tube out. That happened twice. Don tried to write on a pad again. He wanted to tell me something, but he just couldn't do it. He became frustrated and threw the tablet down. The doctor pulled me aside. We need to put Don in a drug induced coma. If he pulls out the tube one more time he will die. We can not put it back again. There is too much swelling and damage already from the two times it was placed and pulled out. Why had he not expressed his last wishes? Why had I not ask? It was too late now. Now it was all on my shoulders to decide what to do. I sat there for a few minutes and told them to give him the mediation. Do whatever it takes to save him. Don was put into the coma. The machine went to work and did the breathing for him. He was now resting. The strong beautiful man I had met just 3 short years ago did not look the same. My sweet husband had tubes supporting him everywhere. I could not see that smile or those big beautiful brown eyes anymore. The family started to arrive. There were so many who loved Don. Both Don and I came from large families, so there were too many to see him. Nurses brought cards and hung them on the wall in front of Don's bed. I begged God to heal my husband. I begged him to save him. Once he was stabilized I was made to go home. No one was allowed to be in the ICU for more than 15 minutes at a time. I kissed him and left for home. It was late and family had already arrived. I went to bed with a stuffed teddy bear covered with Don's robe. I needed to smell him. I finally went to sleep.

Again the Phone Rang

It was around 2:30 am. My sister Brenda was with me. The sound of that phone ripped through the dark room like a bolt of lightning. I sat straight up in bed. I searched for the phone in sleep deprived haze. I finally found it. Hello, "I said." The nurse on the other end of the line said hello is this Mrs. Johnson? Yes I replied it is. The nurse told me Don's heart had stopped and they were working on him. I needed to come as soon as I could. I told her I was on my way. My sister was already dressed. I jumped into my clothes and away I went. I arrived to the hospital and parked just outside the ICU entrance. I did not see the sign that told me I had to move my car by 7am. I ran into the hospital to ICU. The hallway seemed darker than usual and was so quiet. When I approached those big green double doors to the ICU they opened automatically but it sounded as though thunder itself had pushed them open. The noise ripped through the silence in the unit and echoed down the hallway. Once again there were nurses and doctors all around the bed where Don was lying. A nurse greeted me and told me they are trying to get Don stabilized so I needed to wait and allow the doctors to work on Don. I cried I paced the floors. I prayed. The nurse finally came to get me. They had Don's heart beating again. He was still in a drug induced coma, but he was now stabilized. I was finally able to be with him. I was emotionally and physically drained. I sat beside Don and did not move.

At 6:30 am the nurse came to me and told me my car was being towed. Not now! I ran outside and the police offer had my car already on the tow truck. I was sobbing and begging. Please don't do this. I need my car. Please I parked here last night when they called me to come for my husband. I told the policeman my husband was in the ICU and had almost died. He stood there and looked at me. Then he said in a condescending tone. If that's true why are you out here right now. Sir please I said my husband is in ICU. The nurse told me what you were doing. I have 2 small babies and I need to be able to get to this hospital. Please you can call the hospital or I can have the nurse come out here. Please don't do this. Finally he stopped writing on his tablet and then he told the tow truck driver to put down the car. He then told me I needed to move my car. I thanked him for the gift. My sister moved my car. I went back to the ICU.

For the next four days I lived at that ICU beside Don. I was not going to leave him again. I sat beside him. The nurses arranged for a lounge chair to sit at the foot of the bed for me to sit in and sleep if I could. I spent the time with Don bathing him, brushing his teeth and cleaning out his mouth. I did anything the nurses would allow me to do to care for him. I told him I loved him over and over. He was in a coma but I was told he would be able to hear me, so I talked to him. I told him everything I was doing or going to do for him. I told him about the children and what was going on around him. I did not go home for over 4 days. I didn't leave his side. By the end of the fourth day the nurses and my family talked me into going home for a while even if it was only long enough to take a bath and change my clothes. I needed to see the kids and eat a meal. I didn't want to but I left. I was assured by the nurses Don would be taken care of and they would call me right away if there were any changes.

I drove to my sister- in -law, Joanne's house instead of going home. It was closer and the kids were there. I ate the first real home cooked meal in over a week. I took a shower and then sat down on the couch and played with my babies. It was so good to see their little faces. I was glad they were too young to know what was really going on. They knew things were different but just didn't understand. I stretched out on the couch and watched them play. Joanne was a baby sitter so there were children everywhere. It was so good to hear them laugh and play. It felt good to my soul to be here in this place. I felt relaxed and safe. I remember thinking how joyful it was not to have to worry about anything when your a baby. I fell asleep. I slept there in middle of all the noise of the children and the TV.

Death Came Calling

Once again the phone call came. Joanne answered the phone. She came to me and gave me the phone. The nurse on the other end once again told me I needed to come back to the hospital. I was only gone for a couple of hours. Why had I left?! She would not give me any details. I kissed and hugged the kids and left. All the way there I prayed to God not to take my husband from me. I was so angry at myself. I should not have left him. Each time I left his side something went horribly wrong and he got worse! Finally I was back at his side. There were tubes everywhere but Don seemed somehow different to me. I was told Don had a massive stroke. There was nothing else they could do for him. The doctor took me into a private room. There he explained what had taken place. He told me there were no brain waves. Don was gone except for the beating heart and the tubes that did the breathing for him. The doctor proceeded to tell me we can keep him alive but he is brain dead. It was now my decision to keep Don on life support or pull the life support away. My husband was gone and I never got to say goodbye. I wanted to die with him. How will I ever be able to make it without Don. I ask the doctor if he was sure there was nothing else we could do? Are you sure he is gone? What do I do now? The doctor was so kind to me. I then ask the doctor what would happen when the life supporting equipment was taken away. The doctor told me Don would not die right then and there. His heart will take a little while to stop, but we have no idea how long that will be. It just can't be real. This is a nightmare and I will wake up soon! It was no dream. I made the decision to remove all the life supports. The staff gave me the option to stay there in ICU or have Don moved to the oncology floor. The staff there had become like family and I knew they would take care of all of us. I made the decision to move him. Don was moved back onto the oncology floor. The nurses made arrangements for us to have the last room on the right at the end of the East hallway. They also set the family visiting room just outside of Don's room as our place to be together. We had to sit there and wait on Don's heart to stop. I went in and out of his room. I cried and begged God to heal Don. God please don't take him away! I left the room so his brothers and sisters could spend time with him. I laid down on the couch. I was so tired. I fell asleep. Don's heart took eight hours to stop. Around 2am a nurse gently woke me up. I knew her. She did her best not to cry. Softly she said, "Cheryl, he's gone." I ran to his room. On October 2, 1980 my beautiful husband left this world to be with God. I would never again see his big brown eyes or hear that laughter. I cried until I thought my eyes would burst! I went to his room. Don looked so peaceful. I stood beside him and held his hand. I thanked him for the two beautiful babies he had given to me. I kissed his cheeks and forehead. The nurses came in and helped me gain my composure. I got up and went outside. My sister-in-law brought me Christina and Nathan. I thanked all the nursing staff for their support. I then went home. I climbed into bed. I was still in shock. I don't remember even how I got home. I curled up in a ball and cried. I cried myself to sleep holding onto his robe I just needed to have his smell around me.

Saying Goodbye

Have you ever been told something was going to happen and yet you did not prepare for it? Well Don and were told he was dying. Neither of us prepared for it. Don never talked about it and he never left me with any instructions or wishes. There was no life insurance so I had no money to bury him and I was left with all the bills to pay even from his business. There was no will. I was 24 years old and now a widow with two beautiful children and a stack of bills. No one could believe I had been left in this position. Don was smarter than that.

I spent the next 4 days with the help of his brother planning the funeral arrangements. I was in shock. The funeral director told me I needed to bring all the clothes Don would be wearing. I remember going to a local mall. I was trying to get clothing for all of us to wear. It was a weird thing shopping. I went to men's department to purchase undershorts for Don. I searched and searched for a single pair, but they were all packages of three. I don't need three pair! I went to the sales lady. Can you help me get just one pair of these please? Honey, she said, "They only come in packages of three." But I only need one pair I replied. The sales lady replied, "Honey it will be cheaper if you get all three, can't he use all three pair? The tears began to pour, and I felt trapped, I wanted to scream! No he can not use all three pair! He is dead! Why can't you see that! Stop calling me honey! I ran from the store! That sales woman must have thought I was a crazy woman. I fell apart! Why God!? Why God!? Why did you have to take him away? Couldn't you see we needed Don more that you?

I had my brother-in-law pick out all the items for Don. I couldn't do it. I did not want to go into the planning and get in over my head financially. I wanted the very best for Don, but I didn't have that kind of money. So I gave it over to his brother Sherman. There were a few times during those 4 days I wanted to scream, but I remained calm. I could not fall apart I had Christina and Nathan. They needed me to be mommy and now I would have to take on daddy's place as well. Christina was 4 and Nathan was 2. I had to keep it together for them. I attended the wake and the funeral services. I did all that was required of me. I greeted all the people and accepted all the well wishes. The whole time inside I just wanted to run as fast and as far away from there as I could. I wanted to scream leave me alone! I knew if I acted on any one of the voices invading my mind I would simply fall to pieces. So I stood tall and did what was expected of the widow. I smiled and said thank you. I just wanted to go home with my babies and crawl into bed and pull the covers over my head. I just didn't want to hurt like this anymore!

We are told Jesus is coming soon but there is no date. Are you ready for his return? You better plan for his coming! We are not given a date. So I beg of you get ready! Don't be left behind trying to figure out what to do next.

Don did not plan and I depended on him to do it for us. Don was a business man and he was almost 12 years older than I. I just knew he had everything in order. I depended on it. I learned never to allow someone else plan for my future. After the funeral the bills came rolling in. I was given an attorney through the union Don was member of. Don and I acquired a total of 6 pieces of property. There was no life insurance on anything including the home I was living in. It took over 2 years to settle. I lost everything but the house I lived in, but I had to pay for it. I even had to sell a piece of land of was given by my mother. Everything that could be sold was sold and the money was used to pay the bills of Don's company. Don did not incorporate so anything he owned had to be sold to pay off the debt he left behind. Finance's were ruined for me. I was left behind with a funeral and a headstone I had to pay for as well as all the debt he made.

I began to feel like the poster child for Murphy's Law. After the death of my husband I lost 5 pieces of property, and I was robbed twice within the first year. I was trying to cope with loss of my husband and the recurring memories of the rape. I ask God every day, "What have I done? What did I ever do to deserve this?" Why me, why us? God answered me, but I just wouldn't listen. I became cold and distant from my Lord. I was so angry at him. I started calling off work. I couldn't cope. I didn't want to be around anyone. I was sick of hearing it will be OK. I never ask for help from anyone. Two months after Don passed away I quit my job.

God Gave me: Joel 2: 12-13 page 744 of The Way, The Living Bible

That is why the Lord says, "Turn to me now, while there is time. Give me all your hearts. Come with fasting, weeping, mourning. Let your remorse tear at your hearts and not your garments." Return to the Lord your God, for he is gracious and merciful. He is not easily angered; he is full of kindness, and anxious not to punish you.

We are not told the day the hour or the minute of Jesus returning, but he surely will return for us. We must be ready at any second for the Lord to come for us. I will be ready for it. In fact I long for it. I want nothing more than to see my Jesus. My heart fills with joy at the very thought of his return. I will be ready for this. Praise the Lord! Are you ready?

Seasons of Darkness

We all go through seasons of darkness; when anything that can go wrong; can and does go wrong. Jesus wants to enter into the darkness and help us through. The thing is we must ask for the help. I have endured many seasons of utter darkness during my life. Some tell me they would not have made it through even one of my testimonies. How have I gotten through so many hard ones? What kept you going? My answer has always been through the help of my God; My Savior Jesus Christ. But, even when I said it I didn't trust it. How in the world could I say that I know that Jesus is love and that he does care for me, but still need to be in control of each and every situation? I realized I was scared and had been hurt so badly by so many I just didn't trust anyone or anything. I especially did not trust men. After all I trusted my father, my grandfather, cousin, husband and many others, and each of them had destroyed me. Each one hurt me differently.

I endured hunger and sexual abuse as a child. There were cold winter nights with rain and snow blowing into my room and on my bed. Summers went without shoes on my feet. I had a father who worked me and my siblings like adults and never showed much affection. He never told me he loved me. My mother had been so mentally and physically abused all of her life she just wasn't there for me. She was always at home, but stayed in her room. There were no grandparents to offer lesions on life or to comfort me. I watched my mother become more and more depressed. I saw my mother have two nervous breakdowns and being carried out of our house kicking and screaming by police

95

to the mental hospital. I watched them take her away in the back of the police car. My mother was a beautiful woman who married too young and then gave birth to eight children in less than 10 years. Most of those births were at home with no medical help. My visits to the mental hospital consisted of standing out the building looking and waving at her through her bedroom window. During the weeks she was gone all the responsibility fell upon me to care for my siblings and the house. There was one trip when we were all farmed out to the family. That was the worst! We were all split up and our mother was gone.

Mom did not have any friends so she depended on me more and more. Mom told the story many times that I was her only friend and that never knew what it was like to be a child. Mom and I grew up together. My childhood was used to take care of my siblings and in many ways my mother. I cleaned house, watched the kids, cooked when had food to cook, washed dishes and clothes. Many times I took care of mom. I loved my mother so much, but I also grew to resent her. I needed a mother, someone to help me not the other way around! Once mom got a job I barely saw her. When she did come home she went to bed. The job was her get away.

A New View

Once I was entered high school I began to see how other families functioned. They were noting like ours. I saw fathers who worked every day and came home to their wives and children gladly. They kissed and told them they loved them. They ate dinner together. They actually had food like fruits and vegetables. I saw mothers who gave hugs and kisses. Homes were clean and neat. Children had beds with matching sheets and blankets. There was another life and I was going to have that. I hated to go home from those places. Going home was like going into darkness. I just never understood why we had to live like that. I wanted what the others had so badly.

The New Addition

Sometime during my middle school years my father added a bathroom and a bedroom to the little blue house. Our house now had 5 rooms. We no longer had to go out back to the outhouse to use the bathroom. We didn't have to worry about snakes and other animals during the night. At a later time he added 2 more bedrooms. Those bedrooms consisted of a two room shack located at the end of the holler. The shack had no sheetrock and the roof leaked. It was old looking grey boards. You literally see through cracks in the walls. Dad made arrangements with uncles and other men to help with placement. A dozer was brought to the holler and the shack was pulled down the single lane gravel road. That was an exciting day for everyone. It was a site to see. There were very few exciting days for us! I watched as my uncles positioned the little shack against the back of our house. Once it was attached a door was cut into the room. It was a happy day. There was lots of food and laughter all around. We now had two more bedrooms, but there was no way to eat them. We only had two beds to share between 8 kids. It was great to now have 2 more rooms. Four girls slept in one bed and four boys slept in the other. During the winter months a curtain was hung over the doorway that connected the two buildings. It kept the cold from blowing it to the rest of the house. The little black pot belly stove could not heat the other rooms. There were many winter nights that snow actually blew in on our beds. To stay warm we huddled together under the mattress for warmth. It was a miserably way to sleep.

It was too cold to get up, so many nights one of the sisters would wet in the bed.

When I was 13 years old I talked my mother into letting me put a twin bed in the tiny room just between the living room and their bedroom. There was no door and no privacy, but I had my own bed. I was happy. It is so amazing how so little can bring such joy. I had my own space. I was learning new things and meeting new people. I could see the light at the end of the tunnel. I had hope and I wanted out of that place as fast as I could. I wanted a better way of life. I grabbed onto that ray of hope and I never let it go!

I attended church every Sunday morning and evening. I attended anything that would get me out of my house! The church provided the transportation for me. In that little white church named Owl Creek Mennonite Church located on Germany Road, I met lifelong friends. I met Jesus and learned he loved me so I gave my life to him.

All my life I have known Jesus loves me and will be there if I just ask him. I only had one issue with it. I didn't trust anyone. I wanted Jesus to be the King in my Kingdom, but because I was scared I wanted to run the Kingdom. I could not trust that Jesus could run my Kingdom correctly. At a young age I had already been sexually abused, mistreated and used. People hurt me and my siblings. They hurt us badly! I needed to be in control of everything. If I controlled my world no one else could ever hurt me again. So even though I loved the Lord and I knew he loved me, I took control! Funny thing; God will allow us to make our own mistakes.

Part Time Christian God gave me this passage. James 1: 14 – 16 page 1076 – The Way, The Living Bible

Temptation is the pull of man's own evil thoughts and wishes. These evil thoughts lead to evil actions and afterwards to the death penalty from God. Don't be mislead, dear brothers.

Part Time Christian

I have been a part time Christian all my life. Until this very year I did not place the God first in all things. You know the type. A part time Christian may or may not attend church regularly. They try their best to live a good life. They show up when called to help, they give money to local churches, and even the homeless on the street. Surely God knows there hearts. God knows they love him. They pray for peace and well being of all those around them, and long to be accepted by everyone around them. Part time Christians fit in. They attend all the functions. They go out to the clubs and drink, they live in sin and have sexual relationships and bring children into the world while unmarried. They chose their own partners not waiting on God to approve. They cuss and speak the Lords name in vain. They go to the club on Saturday night and go to church on Sunday morning. They shout and praise the Lord. Part time Christians have abortions, cheat and lie and even steal. They make all the excuses in the world to justify their way of life. God knows my heart and that we love him. What a load of crap we fill our mind's with, and all in an effort to justify what we have done and why we left the walk with God. I was that part time Christian. I was saved. I gave my life to Christ. In fact I did it many times, or at least I thought I did. I just didn't put him first in it. I didn't allow God to run my Kingdom. What a mess I made of my life! Praise God I have finally got it right.

My Life Rededicated

This time it was real. I allowed God to fill me up with the Holy Spirit, and take complete charge of my life. I ask God to refresh me. I want you to take control. I want you to be the head of my kingdom. I felt a change in me! The changes are astonishing! My day begins with prayer and reading the Word. God is working in me. I now pray for him to fill me up and move within me, and use me to witness for him. God is working in me. I have been given poems and songs. This very book is a result of his leadership. I have read the Bible completely from front to back, and did it in less than 2 months. I feel a peace I have never know before. God is moving in and through me. I know there are trials to come my way, but this time God is at the controls. I do nothing before I pray about it and ask for his guidance. God gives me the very words that flow from my mouth. He is guiding me and I Praise him for it!

I have attended church all my life and listened to the sermons. I was told God loves you. Turn your life over to Jesus and allow him to lead you and work through you. I just never really understood the message. I made the decision to lead my own life, but ask God for help along the way. I have heard this saying many times, "If you want to hear God laugh just tell him your plans." I personally don't think God laughs much about our plans without him in control. We are weak minded sinners and are easily swayed. When we allow ourselves to be in control we soon lose the vision and the path God chose for us.

Praise God he just now gave me an example of what happens when we walk away from him. There is a large diamond party ring in front of me on the table form a recent party I attended for my great niece. It lights up when the stone is twisted. It really is bright! I picked up the ring and turned it on. I held the ring close to the page I was writing on and the shape of a star lit up the page. It was a beautiful bright star! Then as I began to pull the ring away from the page an amazing thing happened. The star still on and shining brightly began to lose it's luster and fade away from the page. Then I couldn't see the star anymore. It was still there but gone from me. This pure and simple example showed me how God fades from my life as I walk away from his light and his mercy. God never leaves me. He is always there for me and you. He will shine brightly through the darkness and guide each and every step we take if we follow to choose his way. He will even carry us when we no longer have the strength to walk on our own. We must pray and make him the leader. We have to read and study his word! He must be our guiding light if we are to survive this world full of temptations.

I was the part time Christian I spoke of. I did all of those horrible things. I am the sinner who is not worthy to be in God's presence! I ran my life right out from under the light of God. I was lost. I looked to the wrong places, faces, and things of this world for acceptance and love. I was never satisfied!

To this very day I can't quote you scripture chapter and verse. I have not been able to study the Bible long enough to memorize the verses. What I do know is this. God has allowed me to read his word; The Bible, from cover to cover. God revealed to me all the horrible things we have done to each other since Adam and Eve were made. He also showed me his grace and mercy. He showed me he loved me so much that he gave his only begotten son, Jesus Christ. He gave me a way to be accepted and loved that no living human can possibly do.

We are a selfish sinful people. God's own laws were given to us not only to obey, but to show us how sinful we are. We were and are still so bad at following the laws he provided he had to send a Savior. Jesus came to this earth as a human and suffered all the temptations we are exposed to. He suffered hunger, unspeakable pain and rejection from his own people. Jesus was tempted by Satan on many occasions; he was talked about and humiliated. He suffered for us. He was nailed to the cross and died for us, so our sins could be covered by his precious blood. All we have to do is ask for him to come into our hearts and be our heavenly father.

The Battle Begins

When we chose to accept Jesus as our Lord and Savior a battle begins for our very soul. Our lives may have been pretty good and then here it comes. Satan really didn't think much about us before we met Jesus. We were already his. We were OK with him! We did as we pleased and walked our own walk. We were in fact walking the road straight into Satan's fire, his very domain. He was content and for the most part didn't seem to bother us much. Oh he daily tapped on our shoulders with temptations and showed his evil ways. Then here comes Jesus. Glory to God! He filled us up with his Holy Spirit. The beautiful bright light burst into the darkest corners of our soul. Satan was awakened by that light! What is this light he shouts! Who let in this blinding awful light he screamed?! Then he hears the voice of Jesus. I the Lord of all have claimed this child! Your hold is no more on my child! Glory be to God! Satan calls out his army of demons. He orders them to attack! Use anything you have to bring the Christian back to me. Whisper sweet lies and promises of glory on earth. Show them fancy homes, expensive cars and lots of money. Place gold and silver covered in jewels that glitter and beacon to them. Promise them love and acceptance by the human race. Whisper in their ears. Tell them God doesn't love them. Give them doubts such as; If God loves you why did he allow all the horrible things to happen to you and your loved ones. Make them question the word of the Bible. Tell them, you don't have to give up the things you love. You have plenty of time before God returns to this earth. Lie, Lie, Lie, to them. Give them the desires of this earth.

Cause them to fall deeply in debt, so they must work harder and harder. It will make them tired and defenseless. Let lust fill them with the desires of the flesh. They will be so busy with all the stuff in their lives they will turn away from God. Make them crave for the things of this world! Satan uses everything to get you away from God. Go get the Christian back! Sometimes it is a full head on attack, and sometimes it is the very soft whisper into our ears. Sometimes Satan wins.

We must put on the full armor of God at all times. We have to pray and read the word every day. We must not allow the whispers of Satan to enter in. The only way we can survive this battle for our very souls is to change our way of thinking. Read the Bible, study it, pray every day for the Lord to guide you. Look to God for wisdom in everything you do before you do it. We have to look ahead. We must plan for the battle, because it will surely come!

How Do I Plan

I read the living word everyday! Pray for Gods wisdom and mercy, allow the Holy Spirit to fill you up. Know your strengths and weaknesses, and ask that God help you change your ways. Ask for help from fellow Christians and the Pastor in your church. We will have to battle everyday through all kinds of temptations. We are only human and we will fail, but we have the blood of Christ to cover us. We have to ask for forgiveness and we have to forgive! A battle I have dealt with all my life is that of excess weight. I love food. There is not a bad cookie, cake, or piece of chocolate in this world. I love the smell of fresh baked bread. I love the fresh baked bread hot out of the oven with lots of butter. I don't seem to have a stop button! I don't know if it is because of all the hunger as a child, or the lack of love, but I just can't get enough of some foods. So I have to plan. I have learned to know the trigger foods. The ones I can't stop eating once I start, so I do not bring them into my home. This is just one very small example. I know there are much worse battles and I have endured many! I survived only because I have Jesus in my life. When you prepare to battle and place Jesus on the front line with you, you will make it through. I am not saying that you won't be hurt or scared, but you will have comfort in knowing Jesus is with you. You have to have FAITH.

Having faith and trusting God doesn't always mean you will get what you ask for! God has his own plans for us. Faith without work is empty. You have to meet God at least half way and participate in what you want out of this life you have been given. You can pray all day for a degree in your field of choice, or that big land contract to go through. None of it will happen if you don't do the work. You have to apply to the school and be admitted into the program. You have to go to the classes and do the homework, take the tests, and only then will the degree be yours. God will put people in your path to help you, but you must be willing to make the sacrifice to get there. You must do the work! You must put him first in your life. Even Jesus the son of God had to sacrifice. He paid the ultimate price for us. He shed his blood and gave his life so that we could be saved.

Jesus is working through me now. He is putting the very words on this page. I pray he allows me to speak what he wants me to communicate for him. I know he is in control of my life! I pray God fills me up with his Holy Spirit each and every day. I ask for the words he wants to be heard to flow from me as a river flows to the sea. I know he is in this book, because I could never begin to write as I do now if it were not for his guiding me. I praise you father for this gift and time with you! I know it is a healing time for me. God has told me it will be a healing time for another one as well. My prayer is that my testimony will touch the hearts of others, and see how God has walked me through many painful fires.

I am no one special. I am not worthy to be a vessel of God, but I am willing to serve God in any way he asks of me. To honor and glorify your name Father is all I desire. I want my journey this far in life to glorify your name. I praise you sweet Lord. I thank you for loving me!

DIVORCE: D – *stands for divide, I –stands for into, V – stands for various, O – stands for origins, R – stands for returned, C – stands for crippled, and E- stands for empty. Divide into various origins returned crippled and empty.*

That is how I still feel. Our marriage failed after 27 years together. The 4th anniversary of our divorce will be in April of this year. We have been apart for 5 years. Divorce was never a word I thought would ever enter my world. Once again I would be wrong. I stood before God with the man I would take as my husband. I vowed in front of God, our families and friends to take this man as my other self; and join as one before God. To this very moment I didn't think I would even include this part of my life in this book. It stills feels so raw and painful. It is a wound so deep, and so wide. I have spent many desperate days crying out to God! I have had days that I actually cried all day long with nonstop tears and uncontrollable sobbing. I have prayed to God to take away the pain, remove the love I feel for my now x-husband. We shared 27 years together. We raised 6 beautiful children together. We had a life together. How do you move on and forget that much time and love spent together? You don't forget the memories. Even now it breaks my heart that we don't even talk to each other. Then came Jesus. He heals and brings his love and comfort. Our marriage from the start never included Jesus. We did not once ask him what he wanted from us. God was never in any of the plans of our lives! I have been told by many people to just move on, get on with your own life! Your X is your X. He doesn't love you and some say he really never did. He does not care about you anymore! Why can't you just get over it? I ask myself these questions each and every day. I pray every day for God to take away the pain. I have been given dreams about my X that are so painful it awakened me like someone threw ice cold water on my face. Why Lord must I be tormented even during my dreams?

One night while I was crying out to God to take away this pain he spoke to me very softly. This child is another path you chose to walk without me. I will be there to hold you as you cry, and I will wipe away your tears. I will offer my Holy Spirit to comfort you in your times of sorrow. I am here for you. Choose me. I will love you. I will get you through the hard times. At no time did he tell me he would take away the love I have for my X, but assured me he would see me through the pain. Love me child and I will in time heal your broken heart. The Lord as done as he promised and I thank him for it.

There will always be the precious memories of our time spent together. 27 years is a long time to live and breathe with someone. No one can take those memories away from me. I still mourn the loss of my marriage, but God has chosen me for better things. I have gained the love of Jesus Christ. He will never leave or forsake me.

It takes three to make a marriage work. It takes only two to make a marriage fail. Now looking back I can see many mistakes I made. The biggest mistake I made was never asking God for advice in the first place! Remember I controlled my Kingdom. I just wanted to ask God for the advice as I went along. I can't give you 27 years of our marriage history. I would never finish it.

Our Beginning

Remember God was not in the planning. He was not the King of my house. I first met my now X husband just 7 months after the death of my husband Don. I met my neighbors about a year before. On this particular day she called me. She knew I was sad and had lost my husband, so she called me and wanted me to come over. They were having a little social gathering and cook out. When she called me I had a really bad headache and told her I didn't feel like it. I thanked her for the offer, but she insisted I come. It would do me good to get out of the house. I had taken some medication for the pain, so I told her I would be over in a few minutes. It was a hot summer day. I walked over to her house and went to the back door where the kitchen was. There were a lot of people there. The music was loud and the smell of barbecue was everywhere. It did feel good to hear the laughter. I walked into the kitchen and met new people. I held this beautiful fat little baby as I sat at the table. He was about 2 months old. He was the cutest little baby. It brought such joy to hold a new life. I didn't have much joy in my life these days since I lost Don. As I sat at the table I looked into the room directly in front of me. There sat this man. He was so handsome. Our eyes met. I felt sparks fly. "What is this," I ask myself. I have never felt anything even remotely like that feeling in my entire life. We both smiled at each other, but I quickly looked away. I visited for a short time and went home. The headache would not go away.

A couple of days went by. The phone rang and it was my neighbor, she was calling to ask me to meet her outside at the back fence. I told her I would. I finished the task at hand and went to meet her. She handed me a piece of paper. On it was a phone number. I looked at it and ask, "What is this?" She laughed and told me it was her brother's phone number. He wanted me to call him. I laughed and handed the paper back to her. I don't call men I told her. If your brother wants to talk to me he will need to call me. She said OK. We talked for a few minutes, I was curious about him even if I would not call him. I ask all the usual questions. Is he married or is he in a relationship? How old is he and how many children if any does he have? I was told he was not in a committed relationship, but he did have three children already. I was told he had been married young, had twin daughters, but they had divorced. He now has a new son. In fact I had held the baby at the house and met the mother of the child. After the short conversation I went back in to my house. WOW he already has a lot on his plate I thought. He is not for me. I have too much to deal with right now.

About an hour later my phone rang and it was him. He had gotten a hold of my phone number and called me. Ok he must really be interested. We talked for a while. He was easy to talk to. I decided I like this man. Once again God was not in it. I did not consult God. We set up a date. The very first time I was with this man the fireworks flew. It was a crazy feeling, one I had never experienced in my whole life. I wanted this man more than I had ever wanted anything. The date went well. I enjoyed the time I had with him and he seemed to enjoy it as well.

About a week later his sister called me. She wanted to know if I would like to take the kids and come to the park with them. I told her yes. I got the kids ready and met her outside. She did not tell me he was coming along for the ride as well. I was excited and nervous at the same time. The kids and I climbed into the back seat of the car, and so did he. When our eyes met there was electricity between us. It was so charged for me I could barely stand it! I felt like there were butterflies in my stomach. I also felt sick to my stomach. I wanted this man in the worst way. It took about 20 minutes to get to the park. For me it was one of the longest rides of my life. I could barely breathe. I needed to get outof the car. I had dated several men but I had never felt this! Once out of the car I walked away with the kids to feed the ducks and let them run and play. He went the other way with his sister's husband. What a relief.

The Abortion

That very day was the beginning of life together. What a whirl wind relationship it was. We moved way to fast. Again God was not in the plans. We started a sexual relationship within the first week we met. I must have gotten pregnant the first time we had sex. I began to get really sick. I had all the symptoms. No I begged I can't be pregnant! But stupidly I had done nothing to prevent it and neither had he. I was in no way mentally or physically ready to have another baby. I felt I already had too much on my plate! I couldn't begin to face my family or Don's family. What would the people at work think? How could I have been so stupid? I went to my GYN and had the test. I was in fact pregnant. About 6 weeks. I called and ask him to come to see me. I told him I was pregnant. He was kind and told me he would support whatever choice I made. He left the choice all up to me. God was never in the plans! I made all the excuses and I made the choice that I regretted for the rest of my life. I chose to kill my baby. I will not candy coat the title. You know the ones, abortion, termination, end the pregnancy, or a DNC. I chose for purely selfish reasons to take the life of our child. He told me he supported whatever decision I made. I scheduled the procedure and it was done. I went on with my life! He took me to the appointment and took care of me afterwards. I on the other hand; I lied to everyone including myself. I could never have told my mother what I had done. It would have torn her heart out. I took a grandchild from her. I took a brother from the rest of my children. I lied to take time off work. There is no way you can do this thing and not have lies! Even now this is so difficult to talk about let alone tell it to the world. But it has to be said. There can be no more lies and be forgiven. I lived with the guilt for years. It took it's toll on me. Every Holiday I think about the baby that didn't get the chance to be with his family. Yes his family. I named him Michael. I ask that he forgive me when I ask Jesus to forgive me. I lived with that awful secret for many years. I have made peace with the forgiveness I received when I accepted Jesus as my Savior. I told my children, and we hang an ornament on the Christmas tree every year with Michaels name on it. People fight everyday for the right to choose to terminate a pregnancy. It is a decision each woman has to make. No one will do it for you. I hope each one really understands the hell you will go through after you do chose to murder a child. This is my story and my opinion because I have been there. I know the darkness you enter into afterwards.

We went on with our relationship and after just two short months we moved in together. We were just 25 years old. I was a recent widow with two very small children, and he was a divorcee with 6 year old identical twins, and a new baby from a previous relationship. None of that seemed to matter to either of us. It was rocky from the beginning. We were from two different worlds and sets of values. We spent a lot of time fighting, but I loved this man. We split up often but we always came back together. Once while talking he told me he wanted me to be his wife. We married on July 2, 1983. I was the happiest woman in the world. Once again God was not in the plans. We did not get advice from any type of minister or Christian counselor. I chose my path without prayer.

A New Baby Girl

Jan. 10, 1985 our beautiful little girl was born. It was another difficult pregnancy and delivery. Having children was not easy for me and she was no exception. After the birth and the recovery time I was taken to my room. When I got to the nursery Tiffany was brought to me. She was perfect. She had the most beautiful skin and the biggest brown eyes. She had thick dark hair. She also had her father's dimple on her chin. The nurse that brought her out for us to see ask what her name was. We had not come up with one yet. The nurse told me she was so beautiful and the said she looks just like porcelain doll; A Tiffany doll. My husband and I looked at each other and that was it. We loved the name. We took her to the room and then went over several middle name choices. Tiffany Renee. Tiffany was an on demand baby. That meant she stayed with me as much as possible, and if she was in the nursery and began to cry, she was to be brought to me. I wanted her to be with me as much as possible. I did not want to miss a moment with her. I loved this baby girl so very much! She did well and we went home.

ICU for Tiffany

Just 10 days after my precious baby came to us she was close to death. She had stopped eating as much and began to turn yellow. She also had a low grade temperature. I knew something was wrong and called her doctor, but had to talk with the on call physician. I was assured she was fine, but to call on Monday and schedule an appointment if her color became worse. Once off the phone I looked at my husband and I went with my mother's intuition. I gathered my baby and her things and we drove her to the local Children's Hospital emergency room. Tiffany had many blood tests and we found out she was so severely jaundiced she had to be admitted to the ICU. For the next 10 days our baby had blood transfusions and light treatments. She had to go through vision, hearing and many other tests. We were told she may have brain damage and any number of other effects of the jaundice. It was a nightmare. I prayed and bargained with God to take care of this precious gift we had been given. She was so beautiful and sweet. She was a good baby. God answered my prayers. She has none of the effects they were so sure she would have. Praise GOD! She was released and went home. They could not find any signs of any long term damage. We took our little girl home.

Our lives resumed a normal routine. After six weeks I went back to work. My husband injured his back and was unable to work at time, so we were fortunate to have him stay home with Tiffany. I hated the day care centers.

There were many issues that entered into our relationship and we decided to split up. I was crushed. I then joined the local church and gave my life to Christ. I went home to God. I prayed everyday for our broken marriage. I loved my husband with all my heart, and I wanted him to come back home to us. I wanted our family back together. There were many reasons for the breakup. Drugs, alcohol, and many nights that he did not come home, and he just didn't seem interested anymore. I was not one to settle. You give me your all or you go! That was the only way I knew. Even with all that I wanted my family and my husband. I prayed for it every day. We were separated for six months. I leaned on friends and my church for comfort. We talked and decided to try to come together and make it work. That was 1986. A few years went by before my husband gave his life to Christ. There were great changes in my husband, but we still did not agree on a lot of things. We fought about a lot of things. At the time it seemed like we were more like battering rams just butting heads for control of the home. I had my King and I loved him with all my heart, but I didn't trust him to run the Kingdom. I was scared and I needed to be in contol. I couldn't trust in his judgment and he could not understand why. We would fight and then talk about it. Then we were good for while and it started all over again. We never agreed on money issues! I loved this man so very much and I did not want to ever lose him. I tried to get him to go to the pastor for counseling. He would have no part of it. He did not need anyone to tell him how to love me or how to run his life! We slowly fell apart. Our finances went out of control. We ended up losing everything. Our home our cars our lives as we knew it. Through it all we still managed to raise 6 beautiful children who have all graduated from high school and 4 have completed degrees. We loved each other and for the most part I had a wonderful man! He always helped with children and anything in the house. He is a good man, and no matter how mad we were he could always make me laugh. He was so handsome and such a gentleman. He opened my car door and helped me in any way he could.

The New Life

After we lost our home we leased a much larger home on the other side of town. It was a dream home a mansion compared to what we had lost, but it also cost three times what we were paying at the other home. It was the only thing we could get on such short notice. I needed to get a better paying job, and I prayed for one. God answered my prayers. I go the job of my dreams. It paid better and the benefits were better. The hours were flexible and I could work from home. This also allowed me to keep the other job, but work it part time. Everything fell into place and we were happier than we had ever been. Then once again the bottom fell out from under us. The company my husband worked for went bankrupt. He lost his job. It was months before he could find another one, and it did not meet his past salary. The benefits were also not there. The bills began to pile up. It was devastating for us. We thought we were going to be OK and now this. I had to continue to work two jobs. That was not the plan at all. But again God was not in the plans either. I now had to work both jobs. There were two cars to pay for and a house payment that took one whole check. My husband and I were now in our early 50's. We could not keep up this pace. I knew I couldn't do it much longer, but I had to at this point. We would lose everything if I didn't. I take full responsibility for my part in our situation.

I was so tired and was beginning to become sick. It was all I could do to work both jobs and come home. Once I got home I just crashed on the couch. I felt the pressure building every day! What were we going to do? My days began everyday at 4:30

to 5am. For my first job I drove 27 miles one way to the West side of town to my first location. Once finished with passing the medications at that site I had to drive close to 20 miles south of town to the second site. Once finished there I drove back to the North side to start my second job. My second job also consisted of traveling all over town to my patients homes. There were a lot of days I did not get home until after 7PM. I loved both the jobs and my patients. I am a nurse and both jobs were very stressful. After a couple of years I was exhausted. It was all I could do to get home and crash on the couch. I began to have pain all over my body. My muscles hurt all over. I was now in constant pain and the doctor could not tell me why. One day at a client visit I started to have this unusual pain in my lower left side. I had a low grade temperature. I just felt strange. I went home and called my doctor and made an appointment for the next day.

The next day came and I saw my doctor. I felt worse than the day before. My doctor examined me and then said, "Cheryl I think you are a lot sicker than you think." He gave me a script for an antibiotic and sent me home with instructions to call if I got worse.

The next morning I dressed and went to work as usual. By the time I made it to the second site of my first job I was not well at all. I was nauseated and the pain was worse. I still had a low grade temperature. I decided to go to the ER. I called my husband and tell him where I was going. He told me to come home first and he would take me.

I drove home and off we headed to the hospital. My temperature was just below 102. I was taken to x-ray for an abdominal cat scan. It revealed I had a severe infection in my lower left intestines. I was admitted to the hospital. I stayed there for six very painful days. I had temperatures over 103 and severe nausea and vomiting. It was so bad I developed a rash all over my body. It looked like small red pin sized dots. The pain was almost unbearable at times. I was told if the antibiotics didn't work I was looking at surgery to remove parts of the intestines. I was so very scared. All I could think of was losing my jobs. What would we do then? God gently spoke to me and told me you have to make changes in your life. You have to get out of this debt. I ask God for advice and he gave it to me. For the next year I heard God tell me over and over. You can not serve me and do as I need you do if you continue on the same path you have chosen. I told this to my husband many times. We have to make some major changes in our life. We can't continue with this debt. I can not keep working these two jobs! I am so tired.

I loved the house and the life we were building, but it was consuming me. I did not want to lose our home, but we could not, I could not keep up anymore. For the life of me I could not understand why my husband could not see I was falling apart! All I did was go to work and sleep. I was tired all the time and in more and more pain each day. We argued all the time about money and how it should be spent. The last year we were together my husband stayed in his man cave in the basement, and I stayed on the couch upstairs until time to crawl up the stairs to bed. We just didn't seem to be able to communicate anymore. I will not give the details of the last horrible fallout we had, but our last fight led me to make the decision to move out. The next day I went and got a small apartment. I didn't want to go alone and I didn't want a divorce. I wanted out of debt. I wanted to leave a job. I needed to rest. In all reality I wanted to make my husband understand what I was going through. I wanted him to understand God had other plans for us.

After work that day I drove home. Once there I called to the basement and ask if he would come upstairs. We need to talk. He came out of the basement and stood just at the doorway. He would not sit down. It was then I looked the man I loved more than life in the eyes and told him I was moving out of this house. I told him I had gotten an apartment that day. I just can't do this anymore. He stood there not saying a word at first. The he looked at me with those big brown eyes. Tears were streaming down his face. He looked at me and then said, "Are you sure this is what you want? My answer was yes. I could hardly believe those words had just came out of my mouth. I loved him so much! I told my husband he could take anything in the house he wanted. I ask that he call the land lord and give him the 30 days notice that we were moving unless he wanted to stay, but I was leaving. I didn't want a divorce and really I didn't want a separation. I wanted peace. I wanted my husband to fight for us. This was the man who always told people just let her try to get out that door, and yet he not only helped me pack he opened the door and allowed me to leave. God told me what to do and I did it. I could not help that my husband did not want to go with me. I guess God did not give my husband the same message. He did not agree with my decision. For the next month we lived in the house together, slept in the same bed, made love, and held onto each other for dear life. I begged my husband to come with me. I even got on my knees and cried out to him to come with me. He refused my pleas. There is no need to give all the sorted details of why I made the decision to leave my home and my husband. Money was not the only issues we had. In my heart I was doing what I knew was what God had instructed me to do. I knew making the financial change was the right thing to do, but I did not think I would lose my husband in the process. The failure of my marriage was one of my greatest losses. It broke me in more ways than I can express. After a year of separation my husband filed for a divorce. The day we met at the court house I talked to him and ask is he was sure this is what he really wanted and his response was yes. In that court house on that day we tore apart what God had joined together. The pain I felt on that day took my breath away. It ripped me apart! The sobs came from my very soul!

My sister Brenda was with me. After the judge announced we were divorced I could barely walk. My sister held onto me. My now X was sobbing as hard as I was. Brenda looked at him and said why. You know neither one of you wanted this. In a daze we walked to the area to get a copy of the divorce papers. The tears were so bad I could hardly see to sign for them. Once I got my copy I turned and looked at my now X husband. What have we done? I cried all the way home. I cried for days. It was all I could do just to function for the next few months. I fell into a very dark place. There really was no one I could talk to. I just wanted my husband! SO I poured myself into my jobs. The days were OK, but the nights were horrible. I made more and more trips home to be with my mother and sister. It was the only way I could cope with loss. Even though I made the change in my life because I was instructed to do so I still did not put God first in my life and my decisions.

I Held on To Hope

During the first year we were separated my husband and I still saw each other. Friends with benefits he called it. I even tried to except that! I was so desperate to make this work I went along with it. For a time I even believed it would be OK. It only served to give me false hope. We spent weekends together. We talked and reminded each other of all the good times we shared. In my mind if we shared this time and it was good there was a ray of hope we could work things out. I wanted to be with him. I wanted to smell him and feel him breath. I was always so peaceful when I was with him, but each time he left it cut me to pieces. To this day I still love him. I actually accepted this fact in Feb. of 2010. We had spent day together the weekend before Valentine's Day. We had a wonderful time together and talked about one of the first times he noticed me. I was in the yard of my home mowing the yard. He and his cousin were on the roof of his sister's house. They were painting her house and making quite a mess as they did it. I laugh when I think about that day. They had more white paint on the side walk and the roof than they did on the side of the house. They seemed to be having a great time up there. They laughed and laughed at each other. It was very amusing to watch. I remember thinking she is going to be so mad at those two. He told me the only reason I came out to mow the grass was so he could watch me walk in those jeans. He laughs every time he talks about that day. He looked at me and said, "I bet you wish now that I had never came across that fence and into your life." The tears welled up in my eyes. I looked back at him and said,

"I am still waiting on you come back across that fence." He just looked away. I could see a change in him. He made no reply to me. We changed the subject and soon he was getting dressed to leave. Once he was dressed he told me as he always did, take care of yourself. I kissed him goodbye. It was always so painful to watch him leave. I never knew if I would ever see him again. He stopped calling me. On that day I ask myself, "Why do you keep doing this to yourself?" Move on with your life! It is done!

I Corinthians 3: 19- 20 Located in the Bible, The Way page 984.

For the wisdom of this world is foolishness to God. As it says in the book of Job, God uses mans own brilliance to trap him; he stumbles over his own "wisdom" and falls and again, in the book of Psalms, we are told that the Lord knows full well how the human mind reasons, and how foolish and futile it is.

My Attempt to Move On

Once again I made major changes in my life that I did not consult my Jesus. In fact at this time I was angry and hurt! I doubted if God really even loved me at all.

On Jan. 4, 2010 I had to quit both my jobs. I had become so sick and in so much pain I could barely function. I felt like someone placed tubes into my body, and was literally sucking the life out of me. Fall of 2009 I had taken 2 months off work, and then returned. It took everything I had to make it through the day. I was beginning to make mistakes. I was forgetting to complete tasks and worse I didn't have the strength to care anymore. There was a lot going on at my job that had hurt me to the core. For a year I had worked under attack for a stand I was compelled to take. I was right to take that stand and I do not regret it, but fighting a battle can drain you in more ways than one.

I made the decision to quit my job, share my apartment with my daughter, and move into my sister's home. I also applied and was accepted into the local university's nursing program. Our mother was very ill and in the care of hospice. Mom lived with my sister, so I thought it would be good to be there and help out with mom's care as much as possible. Again I did not put God first in my life nor ask him for his guidance in the changes I made.

My sister's house was already bursting at the seams. My mother, my aunt, my sister's daughter and son and her boyfriend were also living there. There were 3 dogs inside the house and 3 dogs outside the house. I brought two more to the mix. There was a care giver for mom who arrived every morning around

9am. My sister and her husband run a small trucking business, and the offices were just to the back of the house. People came and went all the time; either to see mom or for the business. It was a mad house to say the least. The dogs were always barking at something.

My sister has a big beautiful home and it allowed for everyone to have their own space, but it still wasn't enough. From the first day I arrived I could feel the tension. My sister's husband was upset about my bringing my little dogs with me. He didn't want them there and he really didn't want me there either even though he had told to come if I needed to. He did not talk to me about it, but he sure talked to my sister about it putting her in the middle. I was invited to move in by my brother in law, so he knew what came with me. My sister informed me that her husband said, "I told her she could move in with us in a moment of weakness and never really thought I would ever do it." I called a friend and she took one of my little dogs and kept her for me. I started looking for an apartment. The added stress was something I did not need. My pain got worse and I started each day vomiting. My abdomen hurt so badly. I gained almost 20 pounds in the first month I was there. My blood sugars were out of control. This also added more stress concerning everyone else in the house. No one wanted to upset the King in this house. He had a way of making life unbearable at times. With all the dogs in that house I began to hear my little dogs name all the time. Scarlet get from under the table, Scarlet move, Scarlet Scarlet, Scarlet! The undercurrent in the house was staggering, and I got the message loud and clear. YOU are not wanted here! My friend took the one little dog. I didn't want her to be mistreated and I thought it would relieve some of the tension in the house. It did not! I moved Scarlet into the tiny room I was staying in. I did that trying to keep her from under foot and in anyone's way. I would go to school and come back to find she had been let out of the room. It was a confusing time to say the least. I began to stay in that room more and more. It is hard to be somewhere you are not made to feel welcomed.

I did my best to help out. I was so sick and tired all the time. I was much less help than I had wanted to be. I helped as much as I could around the house and with mom. I was now going to school every day as well. I had added way too much on my plate.

After being there for about a month I ask what I would be charged to stay there. I told my brother-in-law I needed to know because I may not be able to afford to be there. Now was a good time to ask since I was already there. I was told $200.00 dollars a month. That was what the daughter's boyfriend was paying. I then handed him receipts for over 700.00 dollars worth of groceries I had already brought into the home as well as all the supplies I had brought with me. My sister confirmed to her husband I had in fact brought all those things. I made the comment I know I have not ate seven hundred dollars worth of groceries. My brother in law replied neither did we. From that day I started to notice changes in the house. It got colder and colder. I got the message loud and clear without a single word being spoken. I began looking faster for a new place to live. I couldn't find an apartment in the area anywhere to rent, and I looked everywhere. I ended up moving out and in with a friend. There I was welcomed and so were my little dogs. I went to school Monday through Thursday. After school on Thursday I drove back to my apartment in Columbus and stayed for the weekend. I did this every week. I loved being back in college. I had always wanted to complete my nursing degree. In fact I was planning to complete my degree and then become a missionary. That was my idea not Gods by the way.

Everything I touched that year fell apart. The school messed up my schedule and financial aid. I was always broke and many times the only reason I had gas in my car was because of my friend and her husband! During that year I moved from my apartment to my sisters, to my friends, my other sister, and finally in with a fellow nursing student. I somehow managed to pass all my classes. I started clinical in the fall. It felt so good to be back in the hospital working with the patients and learning new procedures. I was however not doing so well on the testing end of things for the med/surg class. I passed the class HESI exams without any problems, but I did not do well on the in class testing. I failed the class. I was given the highest work performance evaluations and was told the hospital staff really liked me and so did all my patience. I was devastated! I had to reapply in the fall of 2011 if I wanted to continue.

The Bird Flew Overhead

This is just one of the things I went through during that year. As I said I was always without money. On this particular day I had just two dollars to my name. I was scheduled for class that day from 8AM to 8pm. I needed to eat. I am a diabetic. I drove to a local fast food chain and bought two one dollar sandwiches. I would have one for lunch and one for dinner. About 5:30 pm I was sitting in my car waiting on the next class. It was a beautiful day. The sky was so blue and the birds were singing. I decided to sit there for a while to just get some rest and enjoy the view. I pulled out my last sandwich and a drink. I rolled down my driver side window about two inches. It was a beautiful day, but very hot outside. I had the air condition on. I took a bite off my sandwich. I was so hungry and the roast beef really tasted good. I took another bite and then I heard this splattering noise. What was that I remember thinking, so I started to look all around the inside of my car. I looked at the window on my door. There it was; a rather large splat of bird droppings. It was nasty to see! Then I had this sick feeling come over me. I looked down at my sandwich and there it was. That bird had managed somehow to mess on my sandwich through a small opening on my car's window as I sat there. I could not believe my eyes. I through the sandwich in a trash bag and began to cry. I threw my hands up as I looked towards heaven and said, "Really, Really God! What do you want from me?! What did I do to you? What do you want from!? What have I done to deserve this? Why is it that everything I do fall apart? Again yelling to God what do you want from me?" I sobbed for over 20 minutes in that car. I finally gathered myself together and went to class. Yet again God spoke loud and clear, but I did not follow! Nursing school was over for me! My dream dashed.

Thanksgiving 2010

Mom was feeling badly so she decided to stay the week of Thanksgiving at the hospice center. I had the feeling this was going to be my last year of Holidays with my mother, so I stayed the entire week there with mom. It was good to be with her. She was so fragile and slept a lot of the time. Thanksgiving arrived and family came to visit with her. We had a good time together that day.

I moved back to Columbus. My dream of getting my nursing degree was over. I had failed for the first time in my life to complete a goal. It was not God's plan for me. I still did not listen to calling me. My friend and her husband moved into my tiny apartment with me. Sheryl's husband drove a semi and was gone most of the week, so it worked for Sheryl and I to live together. We both were not well and really needed someone with us. It worked. Once again I tried to find a job, but there was always some rejection, but not always a reason given why I was being rejected. I lost over $700.00 dollars a month in income when I failed the class. I was barely able to put food on the table and make rent. I did everything I could to survive. I had no phone, no TV, and no way to purchase my medications. My doctor gave me as many samples as he could to get me through. I had less than $25 to $30 a week to buy food, gas and any other supply's I needed for the home. I did not go anywhere. The apartment was my home but at times felt like a prison. My world continued to fall apart. My oldest daughter and I were not speaking. I hardly heard from any of my friends. It was as if I had died and no one even noticed I had left. My sister and I were not the same anymore so we barely talked now. I was falling into an obis. I was in more and more pain. I began to sleep more and more. I was broken and no one seemed to care.

Lamentations 3: 15 -21, The Way, The Living Bible, Page - 668.

He has filled me with bitterness and given me a cup of deepest sorrows to drink. He has made me to eat gravel and broken my teeth; he has rolled me in asks and dirt. OH Lord, all peace and prosperity have long since gone, for you have them away, I have forgotten what enjoyment is. All hope is gone; my strength has turned to water, for the Lord has left me. Oh remember the bitterness and suffering you have dealt me! For I can never forget these awful years. Always my soul will live in utter shame. Yet there is one ray of help; his passion never ends. It is only the Lord's mercies that have kept us from complete destruction.

God loves you and will never give up on you and I. But he will punish you as he sees fit! I praise him for that punishment and his grace for me. 2010 and 2011 were two years that tested my very existence in this world. Everything I touched and attempted to do was blocked! Absolutely everything went wrong! I was under attack!

Hollywood Here We Come

My sister Brenda and I have always been close, but this year we had become like strangers. I missed her terribly. Our birthdays are March 20th and 21st. This year would be her 50th Birthday. I called her daughter and ask if anything was being done for her. I was told no. No one had really thought much about it. My sister was busy planning her oldest daughter's wedding at this time. I told her it was Brenda's 50th birthday and she deserved to have the biggest day ever. Brenda had never had a blow out party. My sister had been through so much this past year as well and she just deserved to feel special on her birthday. I did not have money but I was going to see to it she had a party. My niece told me she would talk to her father and see what he could do. Funds were really tight at the time and there would not be much money. She told me she would call me back.

My niece called me back a few days later. This is the plan she told me. We are going to use the local school as the place for the party. The party was going to be a night at the Oscars, and Brenda was going to be the superstar of the night. Oscar statues were purchased. Invitations were made and mailed. The party was posted on Face Book to all the family and friends. It was to be a formal affair. We purchased a red carpet for her to walk on. A cake was made with a movie reel that wrapped all around the cake that had pictures of Brenda on it. There was a golden Oscar statue on the top of the cake. Her daughter made the cake and decorated it. It was beautiful. Specialty Balloons were bought. I searched the internet and printed off pictures of an Oscar statue. I made center pieces for the tables. I went to the local thrift stores and found beautiful gold and silver vases. I used them to make large white roses center pieces. I found gold and silver Picture frames and albums. I printed and framed pictures of my beautiful sister and they were to be sat on the tables all around. The caterer was scheduled. It was a dream night planned. I spent days making a movie of all the family pictures I could find. I visited family members I had not seen in years and obtained pictures to put on the video. It turned out great! I was so happy to be a part of this special day for my sister. I could not wait to see the look on her face when she arrived. She had been told she was to be attending a business meeting for her husband and they needed to be dressed formally. The day arrived. All had been perfect and all we did came together. My sister even had a brand new BMW Z4 waiting at the back of the school with a big red ribbon on it for her! I was so excited for her. She had never had a real birthday party and this would be one for the whole town to remember.

I called my sister early that morning to tell her I was coming to get my mother for the weekend. Brenda told me she had already taken mom to my aunt's house. Brenda went on to tell me she had to go to an event that night with her husband. OK I said I will call mom. I hung up the phone and called my aunt. She told me was asleep at the time. My aunt told me mom had ate breakfast and was really tired so she went to sleep in her chair. I told her we had everything ready for the party. I was worried mom would be upset that she was not told about the party. We didn't want her to be hurt if she was too ill to go. Our plan was to take her if she was feeling well enough on the day to attend. As it turned out she was not well enough. I told my aunt to tell mom I loved her and I would be there later to see her.

The day arrived and I drove home to start the decorations. The beautiful balloons were brought in along with all the other decorations. Friends and family started arriving. The tables and chairs were being put into place. The area was filled with excitement and laughter.

The Phone Call That Changed It All

My niece's husband received a call from my sister. The phone was handed to my niece. David told her your mom wants to talk to Cheryl. I was standing there when my niece talked to my sister. I could see Charity was very upset. I kept telling her to give me the phone. Charity, give me the phone! She would not do it. She kept trying to talk to her mom. I repeated over and over Charity give me the phone! I could feel something was terribly wrong! Charity ran out of the building and went to her truck. I went to my car to get my phone. I would have to call my sister. I tried to call my sister, my brother-in-law and my aunt. NO one was answering the phones. I was frantic at this time. What was happening! My niece took off without telling anyone what was going on. Finally I got my brother-in-law to answer his phone. They were at my aunt's house. My mother had taken a turn for the worse and we were told she only had possibly 72 hours to live. The hospice nurses were there and it was decided mom was to be transported back to my sister's house. I ran back into the school. I told everyone there what I had just been told. We needed to pack up everything and take it back to my sister's house. My sister would miss her special day.

I gathered my things and drove to my sister's house as fast as I could. I prayed to God please do not take my mother from me. Please I prayed over and over don't do this. Not now Lord.

I was the first to arrive. Sometime later the caterer arrived. I found my sisters phone lying on the kitchen counter. She was so upset she forgot it, and that was why she did not return any of my

131

calls. I paced back and forth. I prayed God allow my mom to be OK. It seemed to take forever for them to arrive with mom. I was so worried. What would she be like when she got home? Would I be able to talk to her and tell her I love her.

Finally they arrived. There were people arriving. All the decorations, food and presents were being brought inside. It was well managed ciaos. The ambulance arrived with mom in it. The men carried her into the house and put her on her bed. Mom was not alert. She did not respond to us. I was so scared. I can not lose my mother. She is the best friend I have ever had. Once mom was settled in her room we all took Brenda out to the garage and showed her the party we had planned for her. We took her into the family room and put in the video I had made. It gave us laughter and for a short time it took our minds off what we were going to be dealing with.

All the family was called. There were brothers in other states that needed to get here and we didn't know how much time we had. We were told by the nurses it would not be more than 72 hours and she would be gone from us. I chose not to believe that she would leave this time either. Mom had been at deaths door so many times and had always came back to us. The house was packed with friends and relatives. My mother is one child out of 17. Mom was the mother of 8. There are 62 first cousins from her siblings. Mom had 24 grandchildren and 23 great grandchildren. The house was bursting at the seams. She was so loved by all. People brought all kinds of food. As a nurse I knew all the symptoms and I did my best to convince myself she would pull through this. My heart was breaking. I was losing my mother.

At one point I went to mom's bed side and climbed into the bed beside her. I needed to be with my mother. I was a little girl again and in so much pain; only mommy could make me feel OK. I told mom I loved her very much. It seemed as though there were a thousand people in that house. Mom's room was filled at all times. The first night around 3 Am I was standing at her bedside. I looked at and took her hand. MOM I said really loudly! She opened her eyes and replied, "What!" It was as though she had been pulled back. She looked up at me. Mom I said, Do you love me? Yes, you know I love you. Then she looked all around the room. My brothers and sisters came running in. Look mom here's

Boyd, here's Brenda and so on.' Everyone wanted to talk to her and give her a kiss. Mom looked around at everyone gathered. Then she said, "I know you." We all laughed. It was so good to see her eyes, her smile and hear her voice. We all got to say hello and tell her we loved her. Mom looked puzzled and then she looked at me and said, "You don't think I know what's going on do you?' I know you she replied. Once again mom closed her eyes.

The Hospice nurses gave us Morphine drops for the pain and medication in drop form to help dry up the saliva to keep mom from chocking. We had to give this to her every 2 hours around the clock. We set up a tablet and the schedule was put into place. There were many there to make sure she got the meds, but I needed to make sure each dose was recorded. I didn't want her to over medicated but I also didn't want her to suffer in any way. We would and did whatever it took to make her comfortable. For five days we prayed, laughed, we cried, we shared memories, we all absorbed as much of our mother as we could. We bathed and changed her. We combed her hair. We curled her hair and put her prettiest gowns on her. Many nights I slept on the floor just at the head of her bed. I didn't want to leave her.

Illness has a way of drawing people together and we were there in droves. We laughed, prayed and talked about old times. We played mom's favorite music. We were able to see family we had not seen in years. Mom's bed was turned around and placed it at the center of the room. That allowed for visitors to stand on both sides and at the foot of the bed. Chairs were lined all around the walls for people to sit and visit.

The day before mom passed I was once again standing at mom's bed side. I took a hold of her right hand. MOM, I said again in my loud voice, to our amazement she answered, "What?" Mom, "Do you love me?" She looked over to me, and whispered, "Yes I love you." She smiled. I leaned over and kissed her. Her eyes did not look good. I had someone in the room get her glasses. I instructed someone to get all my brothers and sisters. Mom is giving out kisses. We were all so very excited. Mom was so weak and couldn't move. She stuck out her lips and made the gesture to kiss us. My brother Ray and his children were the last ones to arrive home, and they had just arrived. Ray came into her bed side. He held up Destiny Rose so mom could see her. I told mom,

Ray's here. She looked at him and smiled. He was able to see mom and kiss her. It was just our mother's way. She waited until each and every one of her babies came home. We each were given one last precious gift from our mother; A single kiss goodbye. Once again our mother closed her eyes. We spent the night with her. The next morning we all cooked mom's favorites for breakfast. We made sausage and bacon, homemade biscuits and sausage gravy and eggs. We all sat around and talked about the day before. After breakfast I went into her room and sat down on a couch. I pulled out her music CD and others she had so I could prepare some of the music for a video I was working on. People were talking and laughing. Mom would have loved it.

Then I heard it. Mom's breathing pattern changed dramatically. I looked at her and then looked at my sister. I knew this sound! I told them to run and get my siblings. I ran to the head of the bed with mom, and I wrapped my arms around her head. Mom began to struggle for each and every breath she took. Her heart beat became faster and faster. Her breathing pattern increased and it sounded as though someone was pounding on her chest. The gurgling sound was horrible. Mom was drowning on her own damaged filled lungs, and there was nothing we could do to stop it. My brothers and sisters surrounded the bed, some on their knees and some standing. My sister Brenda stood and read Psalms 23, I checked mom's heart beat, one of my sisters was crying so hard she started to vomit, so she ran from the room, and returned quickly. I heard my brother sobbing uncontrollably, while I whispered to mom; it's ok; you can go mom. We will be OK mom. Run to Jesus mom Run! You don't have to fight anymore mom. I love you. Then as quickly as it started mom was gone. My sibling all looked to me. She's gone I told them. It's over. My brother Kenneth jumped up and quickly moved to the door of the bedroom and then looked back. He said I don't care what anyone says that was the most horrible thing I have ever seen. I responded it was also a gift to be with mom when she took her very last breath. He left the room. The rest of my siblings left the room. The hospice nurse was called. I just stood there at the head of the bed. I was like a guard standing there. I couldn't cry. I just stood there while the calls were all made to the funeral home. My sister and the nurse prepared mom for the funeral directors arrival. I continued to stand there. I watched them get mom ready. Just as they completed the final preparations the van arrived to take my mother away from us. I stood there and watched them place mom on the transportation bed. I then followed them and my mother out to the van. I stood there and watched them place her in the back of that van and close the doors. I stood there and then as they drove away I followed them down the driveway. I had no shoes on and the sidewalk was cold. I walked behind that van all the way to the end of the driveway. I stood there and watched the van until it dropped over the hill and out of my sight. It was then I lost it. The sobs were from somewhere deep within my soul. I heard that little girl inside of me screaming, "NO I WANT MY MOMMY! DON'T YOU TAKE HER FROM ME!" I nearly collapsed right there. It was as if the screams were there, but I couldn't get them out of my lungs. My mouth was open but nothing would come out. The tears started to flow and as I started to the ground I felt these strong arms locking under both sides of me pulling me back up. My brothers came and grabbed me and walked me back to the house. They sat me down on a couch. I could hear voices yelling Cheryl stop breathe. I felt like the life was being sucked out of me, I could hardly breathe. I gasped for air! I could hear my sister telling me to breathe and someone wiping my face with a cold rag. Someone was gently slapping my face. Cheryl slow down and breathe. My sister Brenda sat down beside me and held me. I was finally able to gather myself together and stopped crying. I looked up and told them I am OK now. I am OK.

There was no planning to do. My mom had paid for and planned everything. We already had the headstone and the burial plot. All we had to do was meet and put together her obituary. The service came and went too fast. It was over. My beautiful mother is gone. It would never be the same again. I had also lost my very best friend.

Lamentations 3: 32 – 33 The Way, The Living Bible.

Although God gives him grief, yet he will show compassion too. According to the greatness of his loving kindness. For he does not enjoy afflicting men and

causing sorrow. I was devastated at the loss. I knew in my heart my mother was at peace and never had to suffer again. Mom loved the Lord! I realized I had lost my one true friend in life, and I wanted her back!

On one of my last visits with mom I was so depressed at how my life had turned out. I looked at my senior class picture that was hanging beside her bed. In that picture I had long beautiful brown hair and there was a light shining in those gorgeous green eyes. There were no worries on her face. She was full of promise and wonders to behold. I ask. "Mom, Where did that girl go?" Mom smiled; looked at me and said," She is sitting right there. You just have to bring her back. Get to know her again." It sounded so simple, but how do I do that? I felt so lost and I was falling apart. I was spiraling out of control.

After the death of my mother I slowly fell apart. I couldn't focus. I was in terrible pain all over my body. I spent days crying and curled up in my bed. No one called me. Not even my own children. My friend Sheryl and her husband tried to comfort me, but I just couldn't receive it. At the time I was so broken; in every area of my life. None of my family or friends was calling me, and I had so little money I could barely put food on the table or buy my Insulin and other medications. I was broken in so many ways. The lease for my apartment was ending soon. I had no idea what I was going to do.

My brother Ray called me for Virginia. He wanted me to move there with them. My sister was planning to move back to Va., so I told him I would give it some thought. I took the time to go over my options, and I made the decision to move. I put everything I owned into storage. I packed my care and my two little dogs and away we went. Once again I did not put God in control.

Just now as I sit in prayer and study with my Jesus I heard Satan try to creep into my thoughts. He said, "Who do you think you are? How will you ever answer their questions? Who are you? You have not studied and can't quote scriptures. How can you answer someone who wants to know how can you believe in a God who allows little children and innocent people to be hurt. The doubts began to roll in. This very book is a joke. Who do you think you are and why would anyone want to read let alone purchase this book of yours? You are no one special! Stop it I shouted! Get away from me! Get away from me and stop trying to make me feel bad about what I am doing in the name of the Lord. I confess I do not know verse and chapter. I can't quote scripture, but I do know Jesus is my Lord and Savior, and he loves me just as I am. He is the leader of my soul and is the one who commanded me to write this book. I don't need to concern myself with the things of the future. I do not need to concern myself at this time with questions that have not yet been formed. The word of God is truth and he will supply the answers as they come to me. He will supply the words his words to speak! Oh and by the way I am someone very special. I am a child of GOD! He lives within me and he fills me up with joy! God never puts me down and will never leave me. He never discourages me. His very light shines within me and fills my soul. His Holy Spirit fills my every pore and shines brightly in me. So get away from me Satan! You have no place here. God is here and you will not tear down was God is building up! I give all the praise to my Jesus! I chose life!

I have ask myself many times why am I here. What is my purpose in this life? I have no special talents. I listen to voices that sing like angels. I watch people play the piano. I love to sing and I always wanted to play the piano. Why wasn't I one who was given the gift to sing? Why don't I have a beautiful body? I am as they say a jack of all trades, but master of none. God finally, no rewind, I finally listened to what God was telling me. My purpose in this life is to honor me. Glorify my name! I am to be on fire for Jesus!

> *Ephesians 4: 11-13 The Way: Some of us have been given special abilities as apostles; to others he has given the gift of being able to preach well; some of special abilities in winning people to Christ, helping them to trust him to trust him as their Savior; still others have a gift for caring for Gods people as a shepherd does his sheep, leading and teaching them in the ways of God. Why is it he has given us theses special abilities to do certain things best? It is that Gods people will be equipped to do better work for him, building up the church, the body of Christ , to a position of*

strength and maturity; until we finally we all believe alike about our salvation and about our Savior, God's Son, and all become full grown in the Lord--- yes , to the point of being filled full with Christ!

There is no greater purpose for me than to fill myself up with his Words, and to love my Jesus with all my heart, and allow him to fill up my spirit. **My purpose is to fill his promise!** I am to share his gift of life in me. Praise God! I love you Jesus!

When You Speak To Me You Are All I See

God I hear you. You have pulled back a memory of a time you spoke so sweetly; so very softly to me. I heard your voice and it filled me up with such joy! I ran to tell others but they did not appear to be impressed. Once again I realize the words were for me, and I tried to gain acceptance of the women in my church. Surely they would think I was special if I shared what you had just shown me. Once again I was feeling insecure and needed the acceptance of people instead of focusing on you Lord. There are so many times I have missed what you wanted for me, because I sought out the love and acceptance of those who surrounded me!

Just before the weekend of this women's retreat our family received another devastating blow. The event brought up horrible memories of my childhood. We were all immersed in the middle of an eruption of an unhealed and deeply infected pain! The agony could not be hidden this time. Our childhood secrets were out! We had no choice this time. We had to face the pain head on.

The message I received was during our annual summer camp women's retreat. It was also a time to bring other ladies, friends and family we wanted to minister to. It was a time filled with songs of praise and worship, teaching and skits performed by the ladies, eating, talking and sharing our love for Jesus. It was to be a refreshing time in our lives; a recharging of the soul and healing. It was a time to witness to those not yet saved by the blood of Jesus. The message I received was given to me after one of the morning lession's were completed. We were instructed to go out and find a quite place where we could spend time with the Lord. It was our choice on where we wanted to share this time with God. We could pray, read, or just be quite before the Lord.

I walked outside near the lake and stood on a wooden deck looking out over the water. The sun was shining and birds were singing. The sky was blue and not a cloud could be found. The trees were drenched in new springtime colors of green. The trees appeared to stretch out there limbs towards the heavens. At that moment I prayed, "God, There are so many women praying to you at this very minute. How do you know when it is I? Do you even hear me? How do you know my voice? I then looked to the water below me. There in the reflection I saw many different colors of greens. Some were bright and some dark. In the reflection of the water the bright lime green color just burst forth. It was then **God said, "Child, you see all the colors of green in those trees? You see their reflections in the water? When you look at the water the bright lime color is the only color you see. Just like that color; when you speak to me; YOU are all I see."** In all my life I had never heard is voice so clearly. I was filled with unspeakable joy! God had spoken to me. I was so happy I wanted to run and tell everyone. I did go and share what God had just revealed to me during my prayer time with him to a couple of the ladies. A funny thing happened; they didn't seem to be so happy for me. Once again I had looked to people for love and acceptance instead of God. God had given me a wonderful gift and I wanted to share it instead of just absorbing it for myself. Again I allowed the reaction of others to pull me down, and to take away the happiness God had just shown me. I allowed their reaction to what I shared make me doubt the beautiful gift I had just been given. I turned away from my Lords voice. I felt like the unloved child again. I was not anyone special, so why would God speak to me?

The feeling of rejection took over and I allowed myself to believe it had to be true. I was unworthy, because even the pastor's wife didn't seem to care, or put much into what I had shared. I thought; she is the first lady of our church, so if she was not impressed it must not have been real. I was so hurt during this time I couldn't see the pastor's wife was so busy she didn't have the time to really hear what I was sharing with her. She was in charge of the whole weekend. It had nothing to do with me. Satan found an opening and put that message of insecurity and doubt into my ear. On that day I had been given a message just for me, and I allowed the opinions of others to take God's message away from me! I did not realize the value God's message but I do today. God; I thank you for the love you have shown me! You are an awesome loving God.

Moving to Virginia

I mentioned before I moved to Virginia with my brother and his family. This was a desperate move and I did not consult God. I felt I had no other choice at the time. I had to move and there was no other place for me to go. I could not afford the apartment I was living in, and my friends were moving out. I hired a mover, Justin, bless his heart he has moved me every year since my separation and divorce. I have felt so displaced in the past five years. It is as though I have no home. I have a roof over my head but it never feels like home! All my belongings were placed into storage and I drove off to Virginia.

I called my daughter just as I left the city limits. I was scared and already crying. I knew I had to make this move, but I was so sad I was leaving behind my children, grandchildren, friends and family. I was leaving my life! I had to make a change or I felt I was going to die! Christina assured me I was making the right move. She prayed for the Lord to protect my travel and the road ahead. I felt recharged. I told my daughter I loved her and I kept driving. The trip was over 500 miles. I made that trip alone with my two little dogs who sat on the passenger seat beside me. I turned on the radio and drove. The trip was filled with ribbons of road that stretched before me. God gave me beautiful blue skies filled with his master pieces. Each hill I climbed gave me a new painting framed by trees and sunshine. As I descended into the valleys they always seemed to be reaching out to me and welcoming me into their embrace. It was as if God sent angels to make sure I was safe and secure, and that I was never alone. Even in the time I was not walking with God he chose to walk with me! I made this trip in less than 8 hours only stopping twice. The whole trip I felt good.

I arrived to my brother's home and was welcomed into their home with open arms. I was accepted. I was given a room and love. I felt safe in my brother's house. I unpacked my car and settled in. During the whole time I was with my brother and his family I felt I was under attack. I became more and more sick. I was in constant unrelenting pain. It was so difficult I had a hard time just getting dressed. I could barely walk. I had little to no strength, and had a really hard time just getting out of bed. It took everything I had to climb the stairs to spend time with my nephew and niece. I slept most of the time. This was supposed to be a time of moving on. It wasn't turning out to be like that. I was unable to find an apartment in my price range and I had run out of all my medications. I was on insulin and others as well, but the Insulin was the most important to my health. I began to suffer from the severely elevated blood sugars as well. I couldn't get enough to drink and I lost over 20 pounds. My brother; Ray nor I had the money to get the medication, so I did not discuss the matter with him or his wife. I developed other medical issues as well as a result of the blood sugars being over 400. I ended up in the ER on two separate occasions and even though I had medical insurance I was told there was no reason to treat or give me anything to lower my blood sugar while there in the ER if I had no way to get the Insulin once I left. I knew I was in real trouble but there was nothing I could do. There was no one who could help me, so I did not talk to anyone about it. I couldn't find work and housing was just so expensive. The money I was supposed to receive from my disability didn't come as I was told. It was coming, but was late. I just didn't want to feel like I was a burden to anyone.

Once again nothing went right for me. I could see the worry in my brother's eyes, but he had no idea what to do for me. I didn't know what to do for me! I had never been in this shape or this depressed in my life! I stayed at my brother's home for over three months. It was one of the hottest summers they had on record. We had no air conditioning. We went through an earth quake and a hurricane that summer. I really felt I was being broken at every turn I made. I made the decision to move back home again. Here I go again. I could see my doctor and get the Insulin I needed. I did not want to continue to be what I felt was a burden in my brother's house. September 1, 2011 I got up at 5am and loaded my car, kissed my brother goodbye, and started the drive back home. The trip was really hard on me. I was just so sick. My blood sugar counts remained above 400. My vision was now blurred, and I was exhausted to say the least. It was difficult to read the road signs and I needed to drink something all the time. I stayed so thirsty all the time. The trip that would normally have taken me 7 to 8 hours took me over 11. I had to stop almost every hour, so I could rest. I wanted to sleep all the time. I found a little white church and pulled into the parking lot. There I prayed and tried to sleep. I could not sleep so I began the drive again. I prayed for God to get me home safe.

For the first time in my life I had no place to call home! I have worked all my life, raised 3 birth children and helped raise 3 other children. I have always tried to live right and obey God's laws, why am I in this place in this time? I worked hard as a child to help my mother raise my seven siblings. What have I ever done to deserve this!? I felt so alone!

Finally I made it back to Columbus, OH. It was so good to see that Welcome to OHIO sign. I had no place to go to, so I rented a room for a week at the local Motel 8. My friend stayed there and told me it was OK.

When I arrived to the room I was so very tired. I felt like someone had placed 1000 pounds on my back, and my feet felt like they were dragging around blocks of cement. I took the bare essentials to my room and my little dogs. I crawled into the bed. I went to sleep. I did not call anyone in the family to let them know where I was, so I was awakened by the manager the next evening. She told me family was worried and I needed call them as soon as possible. I did finally get a hold of them. They had alerted the police so everyone was looking for me. It had been posted all over Face Book. They were all worried about me. The Columbus police located my car and called the family telling them where I was. To be honest I was so tired and sick I just couldn't care. I made one phone call and told them I was OK. I was not but I just couldn't spend the energy to care! I was eating ice by the buckets now. I went back to sleep. The next day I called my doctor and had the prescriptions for all my some of my medications to be phoned into the local store. I needed this medication to be able to control the Restless Leg Syndrome. I was a mess!

My childhood friend and her husband called me. Sheryl's husband Scott was a semi driver and would be in Columbus, so he had been given strict orders from Sheryl to check on me! Scott came and stayed with me for a while. We made the decision for him to stay in the hotel with me over night. Sheryl would not have me alone. Scott needed a place for the night anyway, and I had two beds in the room so we all made the decision for him to stay. He went out and brought food and drinks back. All I could do at this time was sleep. I didn't want to eat. I was just so tired. I went to bed and slept. The next morning as soon as my eyes opened I felt like an elephant was sitting on my chest. I was breathing but I didn't feel like I was getting any air. I took slow deep breaths, but it just got worse. I have had mild anxiety attacks before, but nothing like this. I felt like I was drowning! I tried to control my breathing, to make it long slow deep and calm. I got out of the bed and sat up. I felt like I was being smothered. I walked outside the room into the hallway pacing back and forth. I walked outside doing my best to stop it. I tried my best to calm my breathing. It was so hot outside it made me feel even more deprived of oxygen. I went back into the room still gasping for air. I told Scott I needed to go to the ER. It felt like we were driving 10 miles an hour all the way there. I could not control the breathing! I spent the day in the ER. My blood sugar levels were so high they would not read on the testing monitor. I spent 8 hours enduring all kinds of testing that gave me no answers. I cried! I just wanted to die! I did not want to live this way any longer! They treated the elevated blood sugar level and gave me medication to calm me down, and then sent me home. Once again I was sent home with prescriptions I could not fill! My friend took me back the hotel where I climbed into the bed and slept for the next two days; only getting out of bed to go to the bathroom take my little dogs outside, or to get something to drink. I was falling faster and faster into the darkness! What was worse I welcomed it! I was so depressed and sick I didn't care! I really didn't at the point. Satan had won! I allowed him to make me feel things I had never felt before. I was convinced no one cared about me! I was convinced my family could have cared less about what happened to me. Satan used the depression and the illness to wear me down, so my mind was easier to get to. He consumed my very mind! I was in bed rolled up in a fetal position. I knew I couldn't survive at the levels my blood sugar was staying, but I was not in the place to help myself at that time! I gave up I was just too tired to fight anymore! BUT GOD, Praise God he was not finished with me! I may have been tortured by Satan himself, but God wanted me for his glory. Satan would not be allowed to take my life!

Michelle

My dear friend Michelle called me. Michelle ask me, "Cheryl are you alright?' I was so tired I didn't want to talk to anyone, but I answered her questions. Michelle told me she was calling a friend and she would call me back. OK, I replied. I went back t sleep. A few minutes later she called me back. Michelle told me she was on her way to the Motel and she was bringing a blood pressure kit and a glucose kit with her. Michelle told me she was coming as soon as she could, because she was afraid if she didn't she was going to lose me. I said OK and I went back to sleep!

Michelle arrived, and in she came with all the equipment in hand. She took my blood pressure and blood sugar levels. The blood pressure was low and the blood sugar level was too high to read. I didn't care at that point! Michelle called a friend that was a nurse and was instructed to call the squad for me. Michelle was told I could go into a coma, have a seizure or stroke! Michelle called the squad! When they arrived they completed all the tests again and the results were the same. I was transported to another hospital. Michelle and her husband packed all my belongings and my little dogs. Michelle's husband took it all to their home, and Michelle came to the hospital with me. On my way to the hospital one of the EMT's was questioning what I had eaten that day. I told him I had eaten a fresh plum that morning. He was very cold and loud. "Why would you eat that?', he ask? Don't you know as a diabetic you are not supposed to eat anything sweet? It was a very small piece of fruit and it was all I had I told him! I told him it was all I had to eat all day. He sounded condescending. He made it sound as though I had done this terrible thing to myself. There was no compassion from him. I was too tired to fight him or really respond to him. I arrived to the hospital and taken inside. Once they settled me in the same man came to me again and was having me to sign some paperwork! I had not notice him before, but I did notice that voice. I looked at him. He was a tall well built man. You could tell he worked hard at his looks. His scalp was clean shaven and his clothes very neat. He placed one of his hands on the bed railing. I reached my hand over and placed it just over the top of his. The words that came out of my mouth did not seem to be mine. The voice sounded soft and gentle. I looked up at him and said, Sir, he didn't respond at first, Sir, I repeated. He stopped what he was doing and looked me in the eyes. Sir, do you know how you sound when you talk to your patients? What do you mean he ask? You come across as uncaring and cold, I said. You made me feel like I did this to myself. I know you I said. Don't be like that. You have no clue what I have been through and instead of trying to make me feel secure in your care, you made me feel like what was happening to me was somehow my fault. You made me feel worse and scared. He answered, "I didn't mean to sound like that." Well you did, I replied. I am like you I said. He assured me he would try to be more empathetic. I saw in this man how I at times must make others feel. I would give the shirt right off my back to help another, but if the voice they hear is loud and demanding who would ever ask me for help? My X husband used to tell me I could cut his heart right out of his chest and never realize I even did it. Presentation of a message is everything!

The staff in that hospital cared for me in a way in which I had never been cared for ever before. I was admitted and treated both mentally, physically, and spiritually. My friend Michelle literally saved my life that day! God put her there just when I needed it! Michelle stayed by my side assuring I was being treated correctly. Once I was admitted she called my children and friends. There was a team of doctors, nurses, social workers, ministers and so on who made sure I was well cared for. I do not recall much from the two and half days I was there. I was so exhausted from the lack of solid sleep, and elevated blood sugar levels. I was also told I had hallucinations during the time I was there. That makes me laugh. My hallucination was actually a paper clip on the ceiling that appeared to be a bug. Remember I could not see anything well! The elevated blood sugars caused my vision to be severely blurred. Some family members will still not allow that bug to die! "Laughing"

I was released from the hospital this time with a full month supply of all my medications. Michelle took me home where for the next 7 weeks they all saw to it I was cared for. They took me, took my dogs in, and never charged me anything for the help. Michelle and her family are true examples of how we as Christians are to care for one another. I will never be able to repay them or their sons. This is a family who doesn't just talk about God's love they act in God's love!

Another Attack

I was healing and I was reading my Bible again. Satan was not happy about that at all. I had been with Michelle for a few weeks, and was beginning to build up strength. On this day I decided to visit my daughter at her salon to get a haircut. Once it was finished I decided to walk around a little and get my makeup done. It was a good day. I left the mall tired but happy to get out of the house.

Once I arrived home I sat at the counter in the kitchen. I was sharing the day with Michelle when I began to feel a burning sensation in my pelvic area. I kept moving back and forth trying to get into a comfortable place. Nothing worked. It began to hurt me as well. I excused myself and went to the bathroom only to find I was now bleeding ad there was a lot of pain. I went back up the stairs and told Michelle I needed to go to the ER again. I told Michelle what was happening and then I left for the hospital one more time. On the way there all I could think of was that I am so tired of hospitals and being sick! Exams were completed and I was told I have a 6 mm thickening located on my uterine wall. I would need to have a biopsy to rule out cancer. Why Lord I ask? Why do I have to keep going through these things in my life? Have I not had my share? How much more do I need to bear? I was in so much pain I had days that I could barely get off the couch, and if I did; I could not stand for more than a couple of minutes before I was doubled over in pain. I called the doctor who has delivered the last two of my children for the biopsy. The first appointment his office did not have the test results from the hospital, so he made me wait almost another month and rescheduled to the biopsy again. The second appointment came. His office staff still did not have the test results, but he attempted the biopsy anyway. He was unsuccessful. He told me I had too much scar tissue built up on the cervix so he couldn't get through to the uterus to get the biopsy. Now I was in even more pain. I was scared to death that I may have cancer. It runs in the family. I sat up and in desperation; I ask my doctor, "Why can't we just get rid of it? I don't need it anymore. Just do the hysterectomy and get it all over with." My doctor looked at me and said, "You help me and I will help you. Lose weight and I will take out your uterus. With that he told me he really didn't think I needed any further testing and told me to schedule an appointment in 6 months. He left me feeling embarrassed and once again I was made to feel like this was all my fault. I drove home crying and frustrated. Once home I told Michelle what had been said to me. She gave me the number of another doctor. I scheduled the appointment for the second opinion.

The pain was still intense, and I was scared to death that I had cancer. I had all the symptoms. One night God gave me this dream. I was shown a large black ugly mass. It was in my vaginal wall. I pulled and pulled at it until it came out! It was as if I was giving birth. The pain got better. I had the DNC and abdominal scope. The doctor could not find anything there. I chose to believe God healed me from whatever was there. Satan would not win again. Each and every day I could feel I was drawing closer and closer to God.

I Moved Once Again

I didn't want to wear out my welcome at Michelle's home, so I called my daughter to see if it was OK for me to move in with her. I was told it was now OK, so I packed up once again and moved in with my youngest daughter. I needed to stay with her, but I was not happy about it. I have always taken care of myself and my children, and now here I am living with my daughter. I needed her help, and she needed mine. It was difficult to admit I now needed to share a space with one of my children. I have always supported myself. Now here I am homeless with nowhere to call home. I don't like feeling like I am invading someone's space. I am 55 years old, living in my youngest daughter's one bedroom apartment. I am sleeping on an old lumpy brown couch, and I have no closet space or furniture. All of my things still remain in storage.

In the beginning we did not mix well. My daughter and I have a totally different way of living! She works third shift and so we really do not see each other much. She sleeps all day and works all night! My baby girl is all grown up now and I am living with her. WOW; that is different! After I moved into my daughter's apartment I became depressed and spent a lot of time crying. I was so disappointed in myself. This is not what I had planned for my life. Where has my life gone? I never ever wanted to be a burden on anyone! I started to slip back into darkness. I went days without dressing, bathing, or eating. I lay curled up on the couch sleeping. I was in constant pain. I felt like I was not wanted even in my own child's life. For the first month I had no money so I could not buy food or any household cleaning supply's. Once again I was out of money for medications. I had to admit I needed help.

To make matters even worse the holidays were approaching fast and I would not have money to do anything for my children or grandchildren. Everyone is broke! I have 2 very small grandchildren and they would not be getting anything for Christmas this year. This is also the first holiday season without my mom. Without mom none of the family would be together. I felt like a fish out of water. There would not be a Christmas tree or decorations. There would not be any of mom's peanut butter fudge! God how did I get here in this place in my life? I was so embarrassed about my situation. I ask myself, "How did you allow this to happen?" I couldn't understand how I ended up here. I have a degree, I have always had a job, and for the past 5 years I worked two jobs, I raised 6 children, I had a home, I had a husband, and here I am broke and alone living with my youngest child. Now I am on total disability. I kept thinking it was all just a really bad dream and I would wake up. Well it is not my dream it is my life!

One night as I lay on the couch trying to sleep I heard God speak to me. In a clear sweet and gentle voice I heard him say, "Cheryl you do have gifts to give your children and there will be a Christmas dinner. You will have a Christmas celebration." I was reminded of the storage box setting on my floor filled with jewelry and other beautiful things. I pulled the box out and started to go through all the beautiful jewelry I have collected throughout all my life. I sorted through all of it. I pulled out pieces of jewelry the kids have always wanted. God told me to give these things to my children now. Why wait until you have passed to allow them to enjoy them. I gave my son his grand fathers ring and an old pocket watch. My daughters were given many sets of bracelets, ear rings and necklaces. I was so happy just thinking about the looks on their faces as they opened these gifts. This year's gifts were from the heart! It has always been difficult for me to part with my stuff, because my stuff was in my mind my identity. As I looked through all these things a funny thing started to happen to me. With each gift I chose to share I began to feel warmth covering me. A light began to fill up the darkness. God was pulling me back! I began to fill joy again! My children would receive more than they ever dreamed of this year from me. I set out all I wanted them to have. I would be wrapping it later. I had to go get wrapping paper.

A week before Christmas I drove to the local store and looked at all the Christmas decorations. Everything was on sale. I turned down an aisle and there stood an 8 foot pre lit tree. It was a store sample and had been marked way down in price. I grabbed the tree, and then picked out the cheapest red, gold, and green shiny ornaments I could find. There would be Christmas in our house after all. I was so excited. I made my purchase and took it all back home. It was late at night.

My daughter Tiffany and I had talked just that day and she expressed she really didn't care if she had anything or not! Christmas was just another day she said. I knew it was not really how she felt. She was trying to make me feel OK about my situation as well as her own.

I arrived back at the apartment and unloaded the items. I put up the tree and decorated it. I wrapped the gifts I had selected for the children. When I turned on those Christmas lights the whole room came to life! There were no big expensive gifts or decorations but it felt like I had won the lottery. I covered the table with a red picnic tablecloth and sat a bowl of fresh fruit at the center. It was filled with red and green apples, bananas, oranges, and grapes. I used what we had and arranged it to make it a happy place. I could not wait until Tiffany returned home from work. She tried really hard to make me think she didn't care that for this year there would not be any decorations or gifts, but a mother knows her child! I left the lights on the tree burn for the rest of the night. It was difficult to sleep, because I could hardly wait for her open that door and see the tree all lit up. I prayed and thanked God for the gifts. I finally fell to sleep.

Morning arrived and I woke up as the key was placed into the door. Tiffany was home. I sat up with anticipation to see her face! The door opened and she walked in. The biggest smile I have seen on my baby girl's face in a long time just shot out of each and every pore she had. It gave me such joy to see her so happy!

The Christmas of 2011 was the best one I can remember. It was pure and simple! God was in it all the way. I chose to celebrate him and he blessed me for it. December 25, 2011 at 7:30 Am I began my day singing Happy Birthday to Jesus. It is after all His birthday, the very reason for the season!

Christmas Day around 6:30 AM I prayed this prayer,

"Happy Birthday Jesus! You are the reason for the season. (Christmas music was playing in the background.) I want to thank you and give praise for the gifts you gave. I thank you for the turkey in the oven, the deviled eggs cooling in the refrigerator, the fresh greens boiling on the stove, fresh baked peanut butter cookies dotted with Hersey's kisses all wrapped for the grandchildren, fresh fruit on the table, and all the food you have blessed us with on this your birthday. Lord you have blessed me in so many ways, and I can never thank you enough! It has been a hard year in so many. This is my first Christmas without my mom. I know she is celebrating with you. I can see her now with her Lord and singing. Father bless each and every one of my family on this day and every day. Father I ask a special blessing on this day for Barry. I miss him so much. I have ask you to remove him from my heart, but he is still there, so grant him peace and good will. Merry Christmas and Happy Birthday Jesus. In Jesus name I pray, Amen."

It was a wonderful day spent watching my children open their gifts. My 7 month old grandson, Jayden, laughed and played with the wrapping paper and boxes; while his 2 year old brother Christopher opened his gifts. We ate the meal God provided and enjoyed our day together. It was a really beautiful day after all! It was one of the best days I have had in a long time. By the end of the day I was really tired so I chose not to go with my daughters to visit family.

Once again I did not hear from my twins and their children. I love them so very much, but it is what it is. They are my beautiful step daughters, but I have always loved them as my own. They have their mother and since their father and divorced we just don't see each other anymore. Once there is divorce children tend to chose their parent's side and go on with their lives. I can do nothing about that. I love them and I always will!

I stayed home while Christina and Tiffany took the babies and went to visit others. I cleaned up the house and settled in to watch one of my favorite Christmas movies. The memories came flooding back. Christmas has always been my favorite time of the year. It is a time to celebrate the birth of my Savior Jesus Christ. It is a time to bake and share with family and friends. I looked back on all the times we as a family went to get the Christmas tree when we lived on Briarwood Ave. We always had a real tree so there was always a mess to clean up after it was brought into the house. We decorated the tree and put up all the lights. I laugh even now at how my husband always fussed about all the lights I had to have outside. He fussed all the time about everything. Secretly I think he loved it, but it became like a tradition for him just to fuss about it! I could be wrong, but it is my memory so I chose to make it a good one. It was a tradition of mine not to place a single gift under that tree until all the kids were fast asleep. Once they were all tucked into bed and I was sure they were asleep the gifts were all placed under the tree.

Christmas Day arrived and the kids would run to our room and scream for us to get up! Santa came Santa came, get up get up mom and dad! Those were such wonderful memories. It is amazing how fast the years have flow by and all the changes that have taken place. The children are all grown with families and lives of their own now. My husband and I have also gone on to separate lives. My mother and father are both gone as well, and my siblings are spread out all over the east coast and southern Ohio. It is the way of life! We grow and move on. I am alone now. The holidays do not have the spark they once did for me, but I do have the love of Jesus.

My Evening Talk with Jesus

Jesus your birthday has been really good today. All the food was enjoyed. The grand babies', Jayden and Christopher had a great time playing with their boxes and wrapping paper. My daughters loved their gifts from my collection of jewelry. Father I am sad that once again I did not hear from my daughters Charmaine and Frankie, but I hope their day was truly blessed. I love them so very much! I miss my family, but it just was not meant to be I guess. All I really ever wanted in this life was the love of my family. I wanted the Norman Rockwell picture of family! That was not reality, so I was thrown into the real world. It can be very cold out here. I pray Father you bless and protect my children and my family each and every one of them. I thank you Lord for the gift you gave me in the family I have had the great pleasure to know! In Jesus Holy, Amen.

My daughters returned home from their visit with their Aunt Joanne. I thanked God for their safe return home. The three of us talked about the day. We talked until 3:30am. We read the Bible together. Hebrews Chapter 12 and 1 Corinthians 13. God gave me the passages I needed to share with them for that evening. God was already beginning to work within me. We talked about old times back when we lived on Briarwood Ave. It was their home. We had such a great time together that evening. Both my daughters told me I need to move on with my life. I have been praying for God to give me the strength to move on and to stop loving my X husband. How do stop loving someone you have shared 27 years with. Barry and my children were my life. Just as I said those words to them it hit me. "They were my life." God was not! I have never put God first in my life! No wonder I am such a mess! I needed to make some real changes in my life!

After Christmas and the time I spent with my children I began to red more of the Bible. I had a craving for it. How had I spent so much time away from my Savior? I fell head over heels into darkness. It was a long hard fall! There were so many things just in the last five years that broke me. I had placed my precious gift of love into the women I worked with and had my heart torn out and cut into so many pieces. I had trusted these women. They confessed their love for Jesus and many times told me I was loved. I actually believed them! I soon found out that love does not mean the same things to all people. I was cast out like a leper all because I took a stand for the right thing! I stood up for us and was placed as an outcast! The women who once laughed and worked with me now shunned me. When I came to work they were all polite but no one talked to me. No one gave me the time of day. At meetings the boss would sit beside me as if to dare me to even talk. Sometimes it was pathetic. I looked at her and thought, you confess to love the Lord and yet you take pleasure in trying to intimidate me in front of all the others. Inside it took everything I had to keep me from laughing at her. I wanted to tell her you can't intimidate me I am a child of God and I did the right thing! You can not hurt me! Really I felt sad for them. You are so afraid to speak up for yourselves, and yet you shun the very one who is speaking up for you! I took the abuse for over a year. At the last Thanksgiving I was actually ask by the director to decorate for our meeting and dinner together. I felt like I was being tested, but yet again you can't break my spirit or my love for this group of women no matter how you have treated me here. Of course I will I told her. The love I had for them did not change because they treated me so badly. It was an honor to serve them in this way! I went out and I bought all the decorations and made the arrangements for the tables. It turned out really beautiful! I had done what the Lord told me to do. I lived by example! God told me to love and I did.

I went through a devastating divorce that tore me apart. Five years later I am still dealing with it. God has given me peace with it and I am thankful. I lost my mother. I have moved every year since my divorce. I have actually moved everything I own 6 times in the past 5 years, but I have lived in 14 different places in the past 5 years. I am currently living with my youngest daughter and we will be moving again in May.

I am amazed at how God can and will remove every obstacle away from you so you can see clearly enough to see him. Praise God! He did that for me! He took everything away from me that held me away from what he had planned for me. God showed me he is the only plan or path I would ever need. On December 31, 2011, I was reading my bible as I had began to do more and more. I was hearing God speak to me loud and clear.

God gave me: Psalms 119:57-61 in The Book, The Way, page 520. "Jehovah is mine! And I promise to obey! With all my heart I want your blessings. Be merciful as you promised. I thought about the wrong direction in which I was headed, and I turned around and came running back to you!

Glory be to God I did just that! I ran back to my Lord. On December 31, 2011 I went to Columbus Christian Center to bring in the New Year! There I rededicated my life to Christ. I chose to put God first in my life. I mean really first for the very first time. This time I got it right! The transformation in my life has been a real miracle. I start my day with God. I now have an insatiable thirst for the word of God. I started and now have read the Entire Bible from cover to cover! I have always wanted to do that! I have attempted it several times during my 55 years. I was never able to complete it. This time it was amazing to read all the stories and to absorb the word of God! I became filled with the Holy Spirit. I pray each and every day God fills me up so I can be a witness for him. I pray to be used for his glory. This very book is his doing, his words. This is another thing I have always wanted to do. I have always known I wanted to write my story, but I didn't know how to go about it. After I had read the Bible I heard God telling me it's time to write the book. I kept putting it off. I used many excuses such as I can't write fast enough, I can't type fast enough, and I am going to need the money to buy the program I need to write it. I went to bed one night, and as I lay there in prayer God whispered to me, "Cheryl get up and go write the book." I did as he ordered me to do and the words just flowed from me. I know it is God for there is no way I could have done this without him.

My prayer is this book will reach out to someone who may be suffering as I have. I hope it will show God's love and mercy and give you the ray of hope you need to pull yourself back up again. Accepting Jesus as your Savior will give you a fresh start in the plan God has for you. I want you to receive the blood of Christ and be lead to allow the Savior Jesus Christ to make you a new person. Allow him to heal you. BUT you must put him first in your life. Nothing works right without the love of God and his leadership with in you. Read your Bible every day. Fill yourself with the Word of God! God has surely given me back my life!

John 3:16 The Way, The Living Bible, page 900

For God loved the world so much that he gave his only Son so that anyone who believes in him shall not perish but have eternal life.

May God bless each and every one.